Sexuality and Relationship: Guide for a Perfect Life

Author: Shabbir H M Tankiwala

Chapter 1

If, time is money, Sex is Life, Sex is arguably the most exciting fun play, the game that humans likes to play as much as they can, as much as life permits them to enjoy, Sex is extremely entertaining and most pleasurable physical bodily activity not just for we humans but for every living species "Wild-Life or Sensible-Life," we all enjoy this most hilarious physical bodily pleasure called "Sex."

Those folks, who in their life time enjoys sex the most, those individuals who in their life time have got an opportunity to have lived a happy healthy Sex life, such individuals "he/she" will always die on a very satisfactory note. However those unfortunate individuals who sadly couldn't get enough of Sex in his/her life-time, were deprived of Sex altogether or had inadequate and insufficient Sex will die with a deep regret.

But, what is Sex? Is it just all about copulating – intercourse, or is it much more than simply copulating. Dear friends, Sex is a lot more than just a male sucking his Peni inside female's Vagina. Most people almost all over the world for ages, they have construed, that, Sex is just an ordinary physical bodily activity, wherein woman drops her skirt down than spreads her legs and allows the man to lie his body on her than he inserts his Peni inside her craving Vagina and that there is nothing much to talk about, discuss and to understand about, most people live with a belief that they know everything about Sex, such peoples have basically trivialised the concept of Sex, I call such people Delusionist, friends the beauty of Sex is in understanding, what sex is all about? You should rationally feel and absorb sexual activity that's when you'll get emotional high and your mind will get the most pleasure out of it.

Sex has enormous healing powers, it generates positive emotions and makes one feel confident. Good sex satisfies your physical urge, which is normal for anyone to experience, Sex is not just physical sensation but it's comforting and relaxing.

In some of the most socially conservative society in many parts of the world particularly in Asian countries, people for generations have lived with a belief that it is a taboo to debate and to ask questions relating too or regarding

Sexuality and about intimate (Sexual) organs of human's body, overwhelming majority of folks feels ashamed or fears to read Sex related literature in open be it at their home in front of their parents or children or in public places, be it Asia or Africa or any other parts of the world, countries with large population of socially conservative Religious Communities are stubbornly insular in their belief they consider debating or discussing about Sexuality and asking Questions regarding Intimate Relationship is a **cultural taboo.**

Few of those eager individual people who otherwise are from socially conservative religious communities and lives as well in conservative society such individuals if at all they want to read "Sexually Explicit literature or Erotic Literature," out of compulsion they will have to read or watch explicit photo images of sexy men and women behind close door or in extreme remote corner of the street in hush –hush manner, hiding and ensuring no one spots them reading or watching sexually explicit material.

So as a result of people not being more frank and open minded in discussing and debating sex/sexuality and psychological aspects of intimate relationship related issues candidly with open mind in open, this is what results in huge majority of people having very scant and incomprehensible knowledge and understanding about Sex. Because of **No** formal sex education and appropriate counselling, people around the world largely rely on bits and pieces of information that they get to read and learn regarding sex from some odd magazines or articles written in newspaper columns, hence large majority of peoples understanding around the globe about Sexuality is mostly fragmented, inadequate and inaccurate, which apparently distorts the thinking and mind-set and makes people more vulnerable to make silly mistakes, which more often have disastrous consequences.

Most of the perpetrated crimes and social ills in our civil society like "sexual violence, force marriage, forced prostitution, female genital mutilation/cutting" etc are occurring due to lack of sexual understanding as well as due to incorrect information and ill-advices with regards to sexuality and relationships.

Sex is an art, only persons with good creative mind knows that sex is an Art, sex has to be absorb and observed with passion and persistence, Sex is science as it has deep and comprehensive meaning. Also from a bit derogatory angle and perspective, Sex has tremendous commercial value in it, yes, nothing in this world sells like Sex does, Sex is truly a global currency, people around the world can make or rather are actually making millions of dollars by talking sex, selling sex and offering their body for sex.

Sex is such a powerful proven unique weapon, that, sex can (or rather has) bring prosperities and wellbeing to humans as well as sex can destroy civilizations.

If sex brings happiness and makes family truly blissful, sex also as well can prove to be and has actually proven to be extremely devastatingly detrimental, as far back we go into recorded human history, for the past many thousands of years, the records speaks for themselves, Sex has a proven to be principle cause of many brutal wars and battles, even if we read mythological literature narrating ancient history, we find that even many ancient gods and goddess as well developed bitter rivalry among themselves, Gods and Goddess became bitter foes all because of intimacy and their extraordinary sexual desire, the history has witness many brutal wars fought between various Gods, Oops, Humans, Gods and Demons none are left behind, there is sordid history of ferocious battles and brutal wars fought all because of women and sex.

Sex has tremendous commercial value, the world over we get to see how sex is a certain recession proof industry, all over the world there are intimate parlours, dance clubs and brothels, young men and women taking plunge into intimate profession of prostitution and or strip dancers, displaying their bodies and also offering their bodies, serving their body to their sex starved customers for them to consume.

Even mainstream commercial movie industry the world over have been exploring and exploiting sex for their commercial gains, as well as our heartthrobs Movie Stars, have become **Sex Symbols** and such an integral part of life of so many diehard fans of theirs, thereby making oodles of money simply by selling dreams to millions of their fanatic supporters (fans) who are even willing to sacrifice everything and anything they have be it "money or even their life" all for their favourite Film stars, Rock stars and Fashion icons. Yes, sex does makes tremendous psychological impact on the minds of people.

But, what is true sex pleasure? Almost unanimous opinion, every boy and girls have common expectation that they want best match for themselves, every girl dreams of one thing that her boyfriend or husband should be affluent, handsome and smart, and every man wants his girlfriend or wife to be most beautiful and have exquisite sexy body figure.

But, I would like to categorically point out that every good looking thing or items is/will not necessarily will be good in real usage, to elaborate a little more, every sparkling and shining stones are not Diamonds. Similarly, Beauty is not always beautiful at times it has intrinsic discrepancies, likewise, girls who otherwise may be looking extremely stunning and prepossessing and young boys and men who may be looking muscular (Macho tough guy) and striking may perhaps in real term and sense might not be alluring and exciting in reality, most or just a few, always, difficult as it is to quantify but it's true that some externally good looking and beautiful people more often than not, they fake their beauty and strength, some of them maybe frigid, and sexually less exciting on bed, potentially may have "low sex drive," many men and women seems to have regrettable social attributes as well as regrettable attributes inside bedroom.

Don't bother if you are not perfect, because in order to gain perfection it often results in you further **messing up** big time with your existing abilities, it may further hold back your progress, it has been observed that in life most people in a bid to sort out minor problems which they are experiencing, they end up inviting major problems in their life, hence, it makes sense at times that we learn to live with existing minor problems that's there in our life. Risk taking at times is rewarding but sometimes taking undue risk proves extremely brutal and fatal.

In our daily life, we read and listen a lot about counterfeit currency notes and duplicate branded perfumes and about fake electronic devices, but, in real life as well, even humans are fakes, most girls fakes their beauty by hiding the dark circles and black and dark spots on her body with the help of cosmetic products or thru cosmetic surgery, to look beautiful and more presentable, many girls and women who otherwise have small of flat Breasts these girls and women inflate their breasts by inserting heavy padding, fitting silica gel or through surgery.

Similarly young boys and men as well to look sexually appealing to have a strong muscular looks, allegedly consumes some specially made medicine tablets or take injection short to overhaul their body and enhance their looks, hence to look Seductive, Beautiful, Sexually appealing, more and more presentable most of these crafty men's and women's resort to some of the most inorganic, or, so to say adopts some of the most sleazy methods and tricks.

Sex is such an emotional commitment-apparatus as it has such an powerful appeal, that it impacts the mind of an individuals to such an extent that person who's hit by sex worm gets completely swoon, he/she gets deep feeling and sense of excitement, even otherwise the most sensible person or even a man who's otherwise mentally sound and have strong thinking power to understand the nitty-gritty of life, but, at times if a seductive woman cast a spell on him than even the most intelligent and brave man can become victim of sexual desire and loose his sense and his thoughts may get disturb, and indulge into wrong doings.

To define "Sex," in different ways, there are many types of physical bodily activity in which men and women, gay or straight indulges in, all too common physical sexual activities are "Vagina sex, Oral sex and Anal sex," while vagina sex without contraceptive could become cause for wanted or unwanted pregnancy, oral and anal sex could potentially cause severe sexual transmitted infection, each different types of sexual activities provides incredible pleasure and delight but each sexual activity may also potentially have tremendous repercussion and harm the health of individuals indulging in that particular type sexual activities, hence, to enjoy sex and to avoid any kind of health hazard, it is imperative to take adequate precaution before and after performing sex.

Sex includes many things you can do, either by yourself or with other people. Sexual feelings are exciting and because they are, it is easy to get carried away. Sexual activities can be everything from hugging to fondling and touching another person. Sexual activities can also be things you do all by yourself, like masturbating or pleasuring yourself sexually. Sex comes with risk as well as pleasures, so it's good idea to think about the risk and what you are comfortable doing or not doing. Think ahead about choices you make. If the whole idea of sexual activity makes you feel uncomfortable than listen to your inner feelings.

Healthy sex leads to a healthy life, sexual intimacy that is enjoyable and pleasurable promotes wellbeing, also vigorous sex life leads to a healthy life as it provides several physical and psychological benefits. Satisfying sexual relationship strengthens the emotional Bond between couples, making them feeling secured and loved.

Intimacy is about being emotionally close to your partner, about being able to let your guard down, and let him or her know how you really feel. Intimacy is also about being able to accept and share in your partner's feelings, about being there when he/she wants to let their defences down.
To be able to share our 'inner-world' with a partner we love, and to be able to share our partner's experiences, is one of the most rewarding aspects of a relationship. Intimacy often doesn't need words, but being able to put feelings and experiences into words makes intimacy more likely to occur. Intimacy involves being able to share the whole range of feelings and experiences we have as human beings - pain and sadness, as well as happiness and love.

Most of us, however, find it easier to share some types of feelings than others. For example, are you and your partner able to let each other know how you feel about each other?

"(Now talking about sex, what do we need? It always requires two to tango.)"

It takes more than a love to sustain a relationship and to make marriage a successful affair, one has to make supreme sacrifices.

Many couples start out their relationship sensing they have achieved a new dimension of intimacy which they have not experienced before. They are in love, it is exciting, and they cannot imagine a greater degree of intimacy. Yet, as the years pass and couples go through some of the highs and lows in their relationship, they discover a series of deeper levels in their intimacy. Each discovery makes the relationship more rewarding and fulfilling.

Ideally, sex in a loving relationship should be the physical embodiment of intimacy. It should come from a place of love and connection. Within a relationship the two are inextricably linked: intimacy builds sex and sex builds intimacy. However, sex also is just a physical act. Within a relationship, sex is the most intimate act, but it can also be an act without consent, an act which is paid for, or a mere physical exchange. A one-night stand is a perfect example of sex without an intimate relationship. Both men and women can enjoy the sex of a one-night stand, but it is a physical act rather than a loving act.

Article title "**The Truth About Female Desire: Its Base, Animalistic and Ravenous**" has very well written about women's desire, here are the excerpts from the article: "**Some of the evidence suggesting that female sexuality is stronger than is typically suggested is based on Plethysmograph (a tool used to measure vaginal blood-flow and lubrication) studies showing that women become physically aroused to a much wider array of visual stimuli than men (even as they subjectively report a much smaller range of arousal). But what of the hypothesis presented by researcher Meredith Chivers, that vaginal lubrication might not be a reliable measure of female desire, that it is a separate system, an evolutionary adaptation, meant to protect females from sexual violence and bodily harm? If this proved to be true, what would it mean for all these plethysmograph studies?**

Now you're at the most complicated part of this whole field, I think. So, let me pause and try to be coherent. OK, so, if that were true — underline *if*—that were true, that is, if there really are two separate sexual systems, one represented by these physical responses and the other represented by the very subjective sense of desiring, then [these plethysmograph discoveries] would be less relevant to understanding desire. But, I think that both Meredith and I have started to wrestle with a simpler interpretation: that the physical responses, registered in the plethysmography, really might well be a measure of being turned on, being in a state of desire. So, with the range of things that she's exposed women to in the lab — that would be straight women watching two women together, two men together, men and women, and of course, famously, two monkeys having sex — both straight and gay women have consistently responded very powerfully and immediately, physically, to all these kinds of images. And I think, in Meredith's mind, that really does represent something about desire.

On the subject of rape and sexual assault, and the fact that, also in the lab, women are responding generally to scenarios of sexual assault. Here's where we get into a really tricky space, so I hope you have space for this when we're talking about desire. No one, no one, no one — not Meredith, not Marta Meana, and not me — is in any way retracting "no means no." That's number one. Number two is, there are different levels of desire and of fantasy, and you know, fantasy and sexual assault in one form or another are pretty common, but does that mean that any of us want to go out and be sexually assaulted? No, it doesn't. The realm of arousal and the realm of fantasy can tell us something about ourselves psychologically without indicating that we really want to experience that thing, far from it.".......

An Article in **"Set at Dawn": Why monogamy goes against our Nature,"** has written about human psychology and attitude towards sex from ancient time even before human civilization had emerged, "From a biological perspective, men and women simply aren't meant to be in lifelong monogamous unions. In "Sex at Dawn," which uses evidence gathered from human physiology, archaeology, primate biology and anthropological studies of pre-agricultural tribes from around the world, they argue that monogamy and the nuclear family are more recent inventions than most of us would expect — and far less natural than we've come to believe.

Before the advent of agriculture, they argue, prehistoric humans lived in a much less sexually possessive culture, without the kind of lifelong coupling that currently exists in most countries. They also point to the bonobos, our closest relatives, who live in egalitarian and peaceful groups and have astronomical rates of sexual interaction, as evidence of our natural inclinations

Marriage in the West isn't doing very well because it's in direct confrontation with the evolved reality of our species. The best way to increase marital stability, which in the modern world is an important part of social stability, is to develop a more tolerant and realistic understanding of human sexuality and how human sexuality is being distorted by our modern conception of marriage. Certainly growing up in the '70s and '80s there were very few kids I knew whose parents weren't divorced at least once. The economic, emotional, psychological cost of fractured relationships is a major problem in American society — with single mothers and single-parent families

You argue that much of this misery stems from changes that occurred when humans developed agriculture, around 8000 B.C. What happened?

The advent of agriculture changed everything about human society, from sexuality to politics to economics to health to diet to exercise patterns to work-versus-rest patterns. It introduced the notion of property into sexuality. Property wasn't a very important consideration when people were living in small, foraging groups where most things were shared, including food, childcare, shelter and defence. It makes perfect sense that sexuality would also be shared — why wouldn't it be when paternity wasn't an issue?

When you have agriculture, men started to worry about whether or not certain children were theirs biologically, because they wanted to leave their accumulated property to their own child. At that point, people also made a very clear connection between sexual behaviour and birth. Lots of people didn't have a very clear understanding of the cause and effect of sex and birth, but when you have domesticated animals living side by side with people, they start to notice that the characteristics of a certain male that has mated with a certain female show up in the offspring."..........

So, before agriculture, sex was relatively promiscuous, and paternity was not a concern, in a similar way to the mating system of **Bonobos**. Sexual interactions strengthened the bond of trust in the groups; far from causing jealousy, social equilibrium and reciprocal obligation was strengthened by playful sexual interactions.

"Women's desire — its inherent range and innate power — is an underestimated and constrained force, even in our times, when all can seem so sexually inundated, so far beyond restriction." "Despite the notions our culture continues to imbue, this force is not, for the most part, sparked or sustained by emotional intimacy and safety." In fact, "one of our most comforting assumptions, soothing perhaps above all to men but clung to by both sexes, that female Eros is much better made for monogamy than the male libido, is scarcely more than a fairy tale."

In modern times, in this era of 21st century's living in digital age, most feminist women prefer to develop and built professional careers over choosing motherhood and rocking the cradle, yes, in modern times women gender is increasingly defining there priorities, most feminist women are deferring their marriage plans if any they may have for considerable long period of time and instead are concentrating more on their professional career and lucrative corporate jobs, contemporary women folks are empowering themselves with skills, also some of the corporates as well before employing the women staff are taking an underwriting from female staffer that they won't become pregnant for certain period of time while they are employed with that particular corporate house.

Scientifically, nice (heterosexual) guys might actually finish last. A study published in Personality and Social Psychology Bulletin recently found that while men were attracted to nice-seeming women upon meeting them, women did not feel the same way about men. Researchers from the University of Rochester, the University of Illinois at Urbana-Champaign and the Interdisciplinary Centre (IDC) Herzliya in Israel investigated a possible mechanism explaining why women and men differ in their sexual reactions with receptive opposite-sex strangers.

So as a result most women are either delaying their marriage plan for indefinite period of time or opting for live-in relationship with no immediate plans of getting pregnant, but many women reconcile to live as single woman for considerably protracted period of time and instead focuses fully on their professional career. So, more and more females are getting married if at all only once they've passed their pivotal moments of youth age, hence it has been seen that many modern era women are getting married at between 38 – 45, now most of these women spend precious moments of their life without sex, well some maybe finding some other ways and means of indulging in other types of pleasurable activities, with lots of feminist women opting to focus on career opportunities and make money, hence the feminine females are just not only depriving themselves of the pleasure of sex, but, they are systematically depriving the Male gender as well of sex, most men cannot find suitable bribes for themselves as obviously female folks have become commodity which is in short supply.

Not getting any Bodily Pleasure! You're not alone: Women today have less time for sex than their 1950s counterparts. And it's estimated that 40 million Americans have what experts call a sexless marriage (having sex less than 10 times a year).A regular sex life is good for your health. It can satisfy all sorts of emotional- and physical-intimacy needs and help partners stay close, says Anita H. Clayton, MD, a professor of psychiatry at the University of Virginia and author of *Satisfaction: Women,* So, why the dry spell? You can chalk it up to a sheer lack of time, but there are a slew of other reasons, too—from weight gain and Perimenopause to technology overload in the bedroom.

Yes, sex is not the only way to achieve intimacy, but it is one of the main and most important ways to achieve intimacy between a man and a woman. Not making sex a priority can cause your relationship to deteriorate. The passion dies out.

We hear it over and over again: The bed should be used for sex and sleep only. So why do so many of us insist on bringing third parties—laptops, PDAs, Law & Order—into the boudoir? All that technology and distraction can cause insomnia and put a damper on your sex life. After all, it's harder to initiate sex if your spouse is hiding behind a newspaper or glued to the TV or if your hands are busy exploring the Web rather than his body. At a minimum, make the bedroom a no-technology zone, Clayton suggests. Then take a hard look at your life (from romance and work to entertainment and family), and give sex the priority it deserves. If you have to schedule sex like you do a meeting, do it! Well, for any of it to work, you need to first start with a burning desire to do the deed.

For a lot of men, his woman is the only place he can go to for connection and love. His woman is often the only source he has. Men have many challenges in the world – and it's important that he has a woman who understands his needs. **Of course** – understanding a man's needs is not about just giving him sex. Men have many other needs, too. **But the issue of sex is one that many women struggle with.**

And, the modern western world has been affected by the feminist movement which has given women the idea *that they shouldn't prioritize a man's needs,* and that includes not wanting to meet his sexual needs regularly. However, the man is still expected to meet *her* needs!

Sex is one of the major and most important ways through which a man gets his needs of connection/love met. Men aren't just asking for sex because it feels good (although that's part of it too).

The emotional infancy of twenty something men — contrasted with the personal and professional focus of women their age — is the result of our collective cultural decision that it isn't taboo to have sex before marriage. In western society so many creative-class young men are "taking advantage of a social landscape in which sex has been decoupled from marriage but biology hasn't been abolished,"

But fertility is a legitimate back-of-the-mind anxiety for many young women, and we tend to imagine (explicitly or otherwise) timelines for ourselves as we try to navigate the limitations of biology.

Article title **"Can feminism Save Marriage?"** writes: "According to new Pew data, the percentage of Americans who have never married is at an all-time high: As of 2012, 1 of 5 adults 25 or over has never wed. In the 1960s, by contrast, the number was just 1 adult in 10. Liberal and conservative commentators alike point to feminism, and the increased gender equality that came with it, as a primary cause or culprit, depending on whether they're giving the movement credit or blame. But lower marriage rates don't mean that Americans today are a sea of depressed, unstable singles. Quite the opposite: There are more single people because we're marrying later than ever before and building alternative family structures. And for many of us, that's a great thing — it means more stable marriages, happier unions, and healthier families. For some others, though, declining marriage rates takes a heavy toll. And feminism may just be the answer.

The threat of spinsterhood has long been used as a warning against women gaining too much independence or power. In 1986, Newsweek published an incendiary article claiming that a 30-year-old college-educated woman had just a 20 percent chance of marrying; by 35, her prospects decreased to 5 percent; and that if a woman was still single on her 40th birthday, she had a better chance of being killed by a terrorist than walking down the aisle. That wasn't exactly true then, and today it couldn't be further from reality: College-educated women are not only the most likely group of women to get married, but they're the most likely to stay married. Part of the reason is that they're marrying at older ages, which means they're more financially stable, more mature, and have more experience navigating relationships. College-educated women also tend to marry college-educated men, which means their households typically have more money and they don't face the same stressors that can destabilize marriages between couples who are living in poverty or even just getting by. And college-educated women are much likelier to delay childbearing until after marriage, which also contributes to more stable relationships. According to a new book by researcher Isabel Sawhill, these highly educated couples are also more likely to have gender-egalitarian marriages and to plan their families, which leads to higher rates of marital happiness."............

Now to understand it from different perspective; It creates peculiar kinds and types of social problems when most women prefer career over family, now, when a woman delays her pregnancies or when she opts to get married any time after her age has passed 38 years, and when a woman plans to start her family after she's reached 40 years of age, in which case that women will experience many kinds of health problems, because once the woman is over the age of 38 years as it is she will be close to approaching menopausal, obviously conceiving child after the age of 40 years won't be without a hitch, but more importantly lets understand it from social angle.

When, if, a woman who becomes pregnant for the first time at the age of 41years, Now, that woman delivers her first child when her age is about 42 years or thereabout, now this woman who becomes mother at the age of 42 years, so, when the woman age will be 62 years old, her daughter's age will be 20 years old, now this what I mean causes peculiar types of social problems, when there are parents and children in our society who have huge age difference between them, if, for example; mothers age is 62 years and her daughter's age is 20 years old, it's a big generation gap, hence, in such a scenario, for a 62 years old mother to discipline and inhibit her daughter it will not be as easy thing to do, hence in such situations either the mother adopts a very aggressive approach towards her daughter, or considering that she's too old and in her sixties in such case mothers find themselves extremely feeble and just gives their daughter a freehand and allows her to take decision regarding her life.

So, in both cases and instances whether of the mother's aggressive approach or of the soft attitude could potentially prove devastatingly harmful and hence the daughter who's at critical juncture of her life at 20 years of age, with no appropriate assistance and guidance from her mother in such cases, young daughters could potentially go astray.

When there is a huge age difference and big generation gap between children and their parents, it becomes difficult to strike chord between them and to balance their responsibilities, as both children and parents can't understand life from each other's perspective, difference of perception affects family stability, losing temper and patience becomes normal thing, children from dysfunctional families and children who are victim of domestic violence, such children under frustration becomes more vulnerable and susceptible to adopt unethical and unconventional methods of life.

To put things in better perspective and to better understand as in, "how morally correct are these new generation women folks in delaying marriage and motherhood in favour of building more secure and independent professional career:" Millions of women who outsourced their common sense and trusted the media, their teachers, their leaders and their society are now high-and-dry. They were told they could have it all **but most can't.** There are three times as many single women in their 30's now than there were in the 1970's. By the time these women have established their careers, many are too thread bare and hard bitten to marry, and the good men are all gone. They are the victims of the most evil, most successful, **social engineering program** in history. It was designed to give women career *instead of family.* But until feminists acknowledge that they are victims of a cruel hoax, they won't be able to salvage whatever is left.

The key thing to realize is that feminism was not spontaneous grassroots social change as portrayed. It was social engineering designed to phase out gender, marriage and the nuclear family. There are half as many nuclear families now then there were in the 1960's. The destruction of the family is part of a larger agenda to destabilize and depopulate society in advance of a thinly veiled totalitarian world government.

Sexual liberation is part of this agenda. Men see no reason to marry now that unfettered sex is so plentiful. I advise women to consecrate sex for long-term loving relationships and end them in 6-8 mos. if marriage is not imminent. Don't waste time on window shoppers. Feminists have been neutered by adopting the male role model and eschewing the feminine one. They need to rediscover their natural feminine instincts. This involves finding a man they can believe in, and nurture, and not settling for less. True love stems from the sacrifice that women make for the person they love. Let him lead and keep quiet about all his faults. But don't let him take you for granted and dump him if he doesn't love you back (i.e look after your interests and needs.)

These days, it's a woman's job to break the bad news, and often the messenger is single herself, offering up her life as a cautionary tale for the good of womankind.

Regardless of the delivery system, the "doomed career woman" narrative is as perennial as any Disney fable, the theme repackaged and resold to each generations.

There's currently a buyer's market in women who are up for just about anything with the right kind of cad, what with delayed marriage (the average age for a woman's first wedding is now 26, compared with 20 in 1960, according to the University of Virginia-based National Marriage Project's latest report); reliable contraception; and advances in antibiotics (no more worries about what used to be called venereal disease). No-fault divorce, moreover, has pushed the marriage-dissolution rate up to between 40 and 50 percent and swelled the single-female population with "cougars" in their 30s, 40s, 50s, and beyond. On top of it all is the feminist-driven academic and journalistic culture celebrating that yesterday's "loose" women are today's "liberated" women, able to proudly "explore their sexuality" without "getting punished for their lust," as the feminist writer Naomi Wolf put it in the *Guardian* in December.

The same feminist academics pooh-pooh concerns about the long-term effects of the hook-up culture, arguing that it's essentially just a harmless college folly, akin to swallowing goldfish, which young women will outgrow after graduation with no lasting scars. As long as they take precautions against disease and pregnancy, the current wisdom goes, it might even be good for you: a sort of rum-spring a for the non-Amish in which you get your girls-gone-wild urges out of your system before you settle down to have babies.

With so many young attractive feminine girls and women giving top priority to professional career, instead of motherhood or becoming wife of someone, hence depriving ever so craving desirous men's appetite for sex, with young women and girls not making their body available for men to be consummated, hence, so are we to believe that most of the heinous crimes perpetrated in civil society around the world are direct fall-out as a result scant availability of females for marriage and relationship for men, and because of non-availability of young attractive girls for sex, if not by fair mean, get it by unfair mean, becomes norm for many monstrous men, are we to believe that because these men's are systematically being deprived of sex, hence these men are forcefully grabbing these feminist girls and quenching their thirst of sex, yes, it is a valid point to assume that most of the gruesome crimes like Rape, molestation, sexual harassment etc, are committed because most ever so desperate men are systematically starved for sex.

The men who perpetrates such heinous crimes like molestation and rape of women and girls, has got nothing to do with their social strata. Irrespective of men being literate or illiterate both are equally responsible in committing such brutal crimes, in fact the affluent class men are bigger offender, it is just as it happens, is that men from underclass and economically weaker section more often gets caught by law for the crimes like rape and sexual assault and harassment, while affluent class men from cash rich background manages to evade his arrest by allegedly manipulating legal system and law, and successfully brushes his sin under the carpet.

The big question arises that by delaying motherhood, and by differing full time relationship and marriage plan, are the feminist women, in a way, risking their own personal safety and security, as many feminist women prefer living single on their own, most also like to indulge in extra curricula fun activities, thereby it also makes them vulnerable of becoming victim of peculiar types of social ills, these are some of pressing questions and lingering doubts in the minds of thinkers who think about, but those feminist women must be having something else going in their mind hence they've adopted more independent path of living and surviving life all on their own.

While in western countries most girls and women complain that they can't find suitable man to marry and settle in life, as they say that there is dearth of good man, the problem is exactly opposite in most Asian countries, wherein men's can't find suitable bride, live alone using the words "suitable or appropriate choice" of bride, in many Asian countries due to skewed child ratio there exist a huge deficit of women gender, hence, difficulty for the Asian men to find a bride.

Even though we are living in 21st century in these day and time of digital age, science and technology has made tremendous progress, but in most Asian countries, particularly India, China, Pakistan and Afghanistan, these four countries itself put together have a combine population which equals to global population share of 40%, in these countries like China, India, Pakistan and Afghanistan, have worse human rights record when it comes to talking about women safety and security, there's rampant prejudice and discrimination against women.

Most family whether affluent class or underclass, in most Asian and African countries particularly pointing out China, India, Pakistan and Afghanistan, wherein the birth of a girl child in family is considered jinx, most parents first and only preference is to have a Son born into their family, the birth of girl child, it is observe that daughters are considered by many parents as liability and burden on family. Some among many wicked parents even go to such extent that they do not hesitate one bit in either abandoning their daughter or eliminating daughter all together.

The gender sex ratio in countries like India, China, Pakistan is appalling for every 1000 male there are only approximately 855 females (according to some estimates), so with such an dismal imbalance in gender sex ratio, it is obvious that due to huge deficit of women it creates a major shortfall of girls and women available for men to marry.

Add to this is that few among many new generation academically qualified and professionally skilled women are reluctant and less inclined to get married early on in their life, as upscale women delays their marriage plan if any for considerable long period of time, such a move and decision of feminine women further causes dearth of women in the marriage market hence it makes it even more difficult for eager and desperate men to find a bride for themselves and thereby remains sex starved for considerably long period of time or in extreme case men's remain unmarried forever.

One among many reason for brutal crimes on streets of many Asian countries cities and town is that most men are deprived of sexual pleasure, most crimes like Rape, vitriolic Acid attack on young females to disfigure their body and harm their beauty, molestation and sexual assault, all these crimes are perpetrated mainly by those frustrated nefarious men who are deprived of sex. Men throw acid on girls with the intention of injuring or disfiguring girls. Men throw acid on female bodies, burn their faces, smash their noses, melt eyes, and walk away as happy men. Acid attack is common in Pakistan, Bangladesh, India, Afghanistan, Nepal, Cambodia, and a few other countries. Men throw acid on girls because men are angry with girls and women for ending relationships, hence for opposing sexual harassment, sexual exploitation, proposals of marriage, dowry's demand. They throw acid on women for attending schools, for not wearing Islamic veils, for not behaving well, for speaking too much, or even for laughing loudly.

Female foeticide and gender imbalance have or is causing major social crisis and law and order problems in many countries, the governments of many countries as well as social scientist and intellectual class have so far failed miserably to find any solution, one among many reasons could be because many lawmakers themselves allegedly are big social offenders, as it is alleged that "most of the women in most hierarchal and upscale social circle are insecure themselves and have to make many sexual compromise to remain relevant in corridors of power."

New generation needs new solutions, if there is a problem, it has to be solved as well, many religious caste and communities have found some unique solutions to the most tangible problem, desperate times calls for desperate measures, so, what many men, do in countries like India and Pakistan is that brothers share a common wife among themselves, brides in India have become trade-able commodity, hence what happens is that one of the brother mostly it is the elder brother will find a woman and get married to her, then that brother will be her official and legal husband, but his wife will also have an added responsibility of serving her body to her husband's other unmarried brothers which in numbers maybe 2,3 or even 4, not only the bride girl has to serve herself for sex to her brother-in-laws but even in some cases to her father-in-law. Social workers says that decades of aborting female babies in a deeply patriarchal culture has led to a decline in the population of women in most parts of India, like Baghpat (town in north-India), and in turn has resulted in rising incidents of rape, human trafficking and the emergence of 'wife-sharing' among brothers.

Such exploitation of women is illegal in India, but many of these crimes are gradually becoming acceptable among such close-knit communities because the victims are afraid to speak out and neighbours unwilling to interfere.

Social activists say nothing positive can be derived from the increased exploitation of women, recounting cases in the area of young school girls being raped or abducted and auctioned off in public.
Despite laws making pre-natal gender tests illegal, India's 2011 census indicated that efforts to curb female foeticide have been futile.
While India's overall female-to-male ratio marginally improved since the last census in 2001, fewer girls were born than boys and the number of girls under six years old plummeted for the fifth decade running.

'We have to do something about it or we'll have a situation where women will constantly be at risk of kidnap, rape and much, much worse'

A study done by British medical journal "Lancet" found that up to 12million Indian girls were aborted over the last three decades - resulting in a skewed child sex ratio of 914 girls to every 1,000 boys in 2011 compared with 962 in 1981.

Sons, in traditionally male-dominated regions, are viewed as assets - breadwinners who will take care of the family, continue the family name, and perform the last rites of the parents, an important ritual in many faiths.

Daughters are seen as a liability, for whom families have to pay substantial wedding dowries. Protecting their chastity is a major concern as instances of pre-marital sex are seen to bring shame and dishonour on families.

So, as there is acute shortage of girls and women in many societies of the world, people are resorting to rather cruel inorganic methods to overcome that rather sordid social crisis, particularly in countries like India and Pakistan the onus on girl who marries and becomes bride of the house her challenges are multidimensional as she has to serve many purposes, not only to sexually entertain her legal husband but also her craving brother-in-laws and some cases even her legal husband's cousin as well likes to take plunge on her body.

Whether such women who are either by choice or compulsion, circumstances compel these wannabe girls "Bride" to offer her body for multiple sex, now a million dollar question is, do these girls (bride) feels humiliated or do they reconcile with the abrasive facts of life, believes that's what they are destine to do, whether they like it or dislikes it but with no choice, these brides spreads their legs and allows multiple narcissistic men's to penetrate their most lethal weapon (Peni) inside their most precious asset (Vagina).

Now there's also another angle as well, to put things in perspective, and take a more pragmatic view of ground reality.

As the advancement of science and technology and liberalization of global economy has opened up many career and job opportunities, hence, the women have benefitted as well immensely from it. Females in many parts of the world since 1990s have outperformed males by significant percentage of numbers in terms of securing corporate jobs and higher position in corporate hierarchy, in many regions of the world women are faring far better than men. Women has secured many good job opportunities for themselves, as well they've become successful professionals and careered women, with all these achievements women in many households have also become the principal breadwinner for their families.

Particularly talking about Asian countries and most socially conservative and insular Asian communities, seeing their daughter becoming successful professionally and started earning more money than her inept brother/brothers, there is significant change seen in the perception of modern age parents. Earlier those parents who use to consider their daughters as burden on them, but now seeing their daughter becoming successful and earning big amount of money. These parents from the most socio culturally conservative Asian communities where they see potential in their daughter, astute or to say selfish parents have changed their hearts and minds, because in some of the households women are the principal breadwinner and the family is overwhelmingly dependant on the income of their daughter. Hence many parents to secure their own interest and to insure that their families do not fall on hard times if their daughter's monthly income dissipate, if so, that would spell trouble for the family.

Hence astute parents concern about safety and security of their own future, many parents subtly and systematically prevents their daughter from marriage for their own selfish interest, this is also one of the harsh reality of feminism particularly in the Indian sub-continent region countries as well as in many other Asian countries, most career oriented women who have good high pay jobs or professions are sacrificing their own interest of becoming bride forever or for protracted period of time keeping their families interest in mind.

Chapter 2

Good physical relationship evolves when there is good emotional bonding, yes, loving and romantic relationship can survive forever only if there is genuine emotional commitment between two loving partners, otherwise it is said, honesty is the best policy, but, in real life no one practice honesty, every other person particularly in in intimate romantic relationship wants other partner to be honest to him/her, but they themselves are not honest, subtly have sly motives.

To win love a man mostly believes that he can win the heart and mind of the girl only if he speaks lie, and by exaggerating his emotions, mostly the men's try to win women's heart by narrating and telling some tragic concocted story/stories, because they know the women by nature are very emotional, once boy's/male's succeed in winning the sympathy of a woman, that's when woman opens up everything for intriguing man, her mouth and her clothes and gives unprecedented access to the man, that's how some or most of the women also gets exploited.

While sex (intercourse) is on top of the mind of every men in intimate relationship or during genuine matchmaking, women per se things less about sex and her eyes are focus more on the pocket of her man, yes, bodily pleasure and sex is not topmost priority for overwhelmingly majority of women, what matters most for women is quality of life, hence they understand the relevance of money power, women in whatsoever types of relation be it intimate illicit relationship or official relationship, women always weigh how financially well-of her male companion is, be it her prospective husband --- lover or paramour, subtly or overtly, what matters most to women and girls is spending power of the man in their life. How much can a man spend on buying her expensive gifts, takes her out for lavish lunch and dinner, picnics and outings? Well, still it is always difficult to define a woman's aspiration and her needs, but one thing is certain that most women crave for Rich affluent man to romance with.

So, there is so much in the world to get, but, yet, there is so little people have, basically because of distrust among themselves, as most people are reluctant to trust the other, and when they do take risk of trusting someone that person outrageously betrays his/her trust, this is why perhaps many people remains deprived of true love in their life, as it is always important that gay or straight, man or woman, in relationship both needs to be honest with each other.

Most of the couples, be it man or woman, normally fakes their emotions and their feelings to each other. High on words, low on substance, whether it's man or woman, both wants best deal for themselves, however they will try to impress upon each other by assuring and saying that how much love matters to them and they are not money minded at all, not after money or any other valuables, it is just true love that matters to them, these kinds of rhetorical language needs to be construed as just an emotional drama, basically both man and woman, or at least one of them is with his/her sly motives trying to exploit the other.

Article title **"Extramarital affairs: 'Economically independent Indian women not afraid to articulate their sexual needs,"** here are some excerpts from the article, which shares opinion particularly on the socially conservative Indian people, how with changing times Indian's too are changing their social behaviour, this article is worth discussing because Indians boast a lot about their culture and family values, let's have a listen, what Indians says about new generation of Indians changing attributes: "There has been at least 30 per cent increase in the number of women indulging in extramarital affairs in the past five years," says Chhabria. Filmmaker Vinta Nanda agrees that there has been an increase in extramarital affairs, but more importantly, people are not judgemental about it. "However, the institution of marriage has not evolved with the world," she adds. Marriage counsellor Ameeta Sanghavi Shah points out that when physical and emotional needs are met outside wedlock, women get addicted to the attention and slowly boundaries get eroded. Extramarital affairs are bubble relationships where the romanticism and adventure are not overshadowed by the nitty-gritty of everyday life unlike with the spouse.

But extramarital affairs are not conceived, "especially when you are 25 and in awe of your 35-year-old successful boss", says a senior HR manager, according to whom careers have taken precedence over everything else for most women.

The economically and sexually liberated woman of today feels confident of dealing with the consequences of her sexual adventures. Though still torn between guilt and search for personal gratification, she does not mind forging a bond with another partner at the workplace. Working long hours in close proximity with male colleagues under high levels of stress does act as a catalyst. The attitude of "if I am not getting satisfaction from my husband, I will get it from somewhere else" is growing among women, says Tulalwar.

The excitement and adventure of extramarital affairs is followed by bouts of depression and loneliness in a number of cases. Though there is no data to prove it, most extramarital affairs eventually wither away when harsh realities of life beckon the engaging couple to ground zero. "In most cases, the accountability to the child is more important to the woman than to her husband," says Deshmukh."......

If today's woman finds that her emotional and physical needs are not being met, she now has the option of outsourcing them, so this is how Indians as well are catching up with their western peers, in fact, are opting to become more promiscuous than western folks.

Sexual dysfunction is broadly defined as the inability to fully enjoy sexual inter course. Specifically, sexual dysfunctions are disorders that   interfere with a full sexual response cycle. These disorders makes it difficult for a person to enjoy or to have sexual intercourse. While   sexual dysfunction rarely threatens physical health
it can take a heavy psychological toll, bringing on depression, **anxiety**, and debilitating feelings of inadequacy.

Women who are promiscuous are more likely to keep their reputation intact if they are high earners, an academic study has shown.
Attitudes towards promiscuity are heavily influenced by women's earning power while people who disapprove of casual relationships are more likely to know women who are in low-paid jobs or rely on their partner to support them.

A woman having sex with multiple partners means she makes the choices, which goes against women as property. It suggests women have desire, always a dangerous thing. Not to mention promiscuity being an easy tool for general shaming and silencing of women (many genuinely think that "but she's a slut!" defeats any argument). When fear of promiscuity leads to psychological damage like **purity balls**, it becomes obvious that it's all about harm — causing harm. Ultimately it boils down to the classic definition:

It defines promiscuity as "sex with series of other adults, not directly related through marriage, with no commitments," (although this definition may not be entirely correct, we won't argue against this definition as it's not the essay's purpose). This traditional view implies that (1) promiscuity has negative effects on marriage, and (2) monogamy is socially superior to the alternatives.

Promiscuity, infidelity, double standards, cheating in relationship these are some of the core reasons act as catalyst for Domestic Violence. Yes, domestic violence have devastating consequences, overwhelming majority of people around the world are affected by domestic violence, domestic violence is unique in nature, it is more subtle and most dangerous form of violence, at times the victim is unable to realize the fact that he/she is/has become victim of domestic violence and is being impacted by domestic violence.

Domestic violence can destroy person/persons professional life, can cause depression, victims of domestic violence often suffers severe financial crisis, sex life and personal family life both gets profoundly impacted negatively, most instances and cases of drug abuse, alcohol abuse, sexual discrimination as well as those who commits petty crimes are often those people who are affected by or are victim of domestic violence.

Article title "**JHM Global Scotland' ending violence against women**" articulate rather well in its report, the reason and causes of brutal domestic violence in Pakistan, India and Africa: "**Domestic Violence in Pakistan**: Domestic abuse & domestic violence in Pakistan is very common. Killing, burning and maiming victims is not outside of the psyche of perpetrators in Pakistan. Extreme violence is part of society and not shocking to see it happen. Religious belief that empowers a husband's beating of his wife does not help the problem at all. Spousal abuse while being the most commonly reported form of domestic violence probably makes up for very little proportion of the collective statistics on domestic violence because domestic violence encompasses all sorts of abuses in a household. It includes child abuse, intimate partner violence (IPV) and domestic violence and other forms of abuse.

Domestic Violence in India: United Nation Population Fund Report stated that:
1] Two-third of married Indian women are victims of domestic violence.
2] As many as 70 per cent of married women in India between the age of 15 and 49 are victims of beating, rape or forced sex.
3] More than 55 percent of the women suffer from domestic violence, especially in the states of Bihar, Utter Pradesh and other northern states.
The violence used in India to treat women comes on a higher scale amongst nations whose culture & religion condones ill treatment of women. Brides are tormented due to dowry payment failure. Women who fail to give birth to sons instead of daughters are treated as useless, worthless and second class in a society where boys are more valued than girls. Many women have been tortured, set ablaze & burned alive, amputated or treated with extreme cruelty by whole families. It is appalling.

Domestic Violence in Africa: Domestic abuse & domestic violence is very common in Africa. Beating women, murder, and maiming victims is not unusual in many respect both in villages & in big cities across Africa. Violence is uncommon place and it is part of the society norm in many respect. War, political clashes & regular tribal & inter-tribal conflict have left a permission mentality for violence to be perpetrated and women are the weakest link and the commonest victims.

Most Common Causes: The most common causes for women stalking and battering include dissatisfaction with the dowry and exploiting women for more of it, arguing with the partner, refusing to have sex with him, neglecting children, going out of home without telling the partner, not cooking properly or on time, indulging in extra marital affairs, not looking after in-laws etc. In some cases infertility in females also leads to their assault by the family members. The greed for dowry, desire for a male child and alcoholism of the spouse are major factors of domestic violence against women in rural areas. There have been gruesome reports of young bride being burnt alive or subjected to continuous harassment for not bringing home the amount of demanded dowry. Women in India also admit to hitting or beating because of their suspicion about the husband's sexual involvement with other women."...........

So, this is how domestic violence is affecting people around the world.

Certain patterns of violence in both childhood and adulthood may make a woman more likely to take significant sexual risks, such as having unprotected sex or a high number of sexual partners, said researchers from The Miriam Hospital's Centres for Behavioural and Preventive Medicine.

Given the ties between multiple violent experiences and sexual risk-taking, clinicians working with women who experience violence or who are at risk for HIV/STDs may need to consider the overlap between the two in order to impact sexual health consequences.

"The clustering of different types of violence suggests clinicians who work with women who have experienced one type of violence should inquire about other types of violence in order to get a complete picture.

With the understanding that multiple violence experiences are common for women with the highest sexual risk, experts also suggests interventionists working to reduce HIV risk may want to provide women with resources for coping with intimate partner and community violence, or for overcoming childhood maltreatment or abuse. Similarly, those working with women experiencing intimate partner violence or other forms of violence may want to address strategies for safer sex.

Racial, linguistic, Religious prejudice, we humans should learn to be more human, in our approach to gain love we must not lose our dignity or should not harm someone else's dignity, some among us humans stoop to low, they are selfish and cunning in their manoeuvre to gain love, more so to exploit others, particularly it has been seen and observed, some individuals or to say people of certain religious groups are so selfish and cruel, these lot of people care little about humanity or morality, for some people playing with emotions and exploiting others has become a habit, while for some even profession.

Yes, I am talking about those people from section of society who have religious prejudice, some wicked individuals and groups of people have such a notion they will protect the dignity of girls and women of their own religion and ethnic group, they'll ensure that their females folks belonging to their own community is well protected and her dignity upheld, but, these same lot of people don't ever mind one bit, never hesitate in humiliating and sexually exploiting females from other religious communities, after exploiting and harming girls sexually these men's never regret for their wrong doings instead they make fun and laughs at the plight of other woman's ordeal, people of certain religious community with pride harms females from other religious communities.

Here I would like to quote a paragraph from an article "**Sex and Sexuality in Islam**": "In Islam, keeping the virginity is the highest asset that a woman could possess. There is no crime/sin as despicable as that of losing the virginity before a woman is married. The thought of indulging in pre-marital sex by an adult woman is absolutely unthinkable in Islam (For men it is a different story altogether. As we shall see later, it is possible for an unmarried Muslim man to be engaged in sex with slave-girls/captive/infidel women but not with free Muslim women). Mind you, premarital sex is a serious crime that may involve severe punishment for the offender; one hundred Islamic lashing for the unmarried woman (or man) and stoning to death for the married woman (or man). This punishment is *hudud*, which means that there is no way the offender can escape the severity of this kind of barbaric torment. Once the punishment has been passed down, it must be carried out at any cost. So much for Islamic mercy and tolerance! If you thought that I am being too critical, then please be reminded that in Islam, homicide is not such a serious offence as sex is. That is to say, the punishment for a murder can be commuted to other sentence like *Qias* (retaliation) or *Diya* (blood money). Now contrast this if you will, with the laws for sexual offences. It looks like that taking a life is much simpler and easier than making love, especially for women, if we go by the Islamic rules. How barbaric and at the same time myopic view!"...... "this is to be construed as wicked hypocrisy, while Muslim women needs to be protected but it is ok for Muslim men to have sex with "slave/captive or infidel women" this is cruelty against humanity. No, the purpose is not to defame or debase any religion or Islam, people from other religious communities as well do such things what Muslim men do, here the purpose of debate is to be honest and learn to respect every men and women without being bias, NOT to have any kind of prejudice in our hearts and minds.

"Women is a Nature's Best Creation, hence, Discriminating a Women is equal to Discriminating Mother Nature."

It is one thing to be academically brilliant and be highly qualified and another thing all together to be intellectually brilliant, I consider those people who have "religious and linguistic prejudice" as inferior and inhuman idiots.

It has been linked to stereotypes and gender roles, and may include the belief that one sex or gender is intrinsically superior to another. Sexism affects both men and women but primarily it's women who suffers most. Explicitly speaking, Sexism is an offensive reminder of the way cultures perceive and treats women. Extreme sexism may foster sexual harassment, rape and other forms and types of sexual violence.

Sex by conventional means or unconventional practice, when libido is high and uncontrollable, peoples patience runs out, they want to have fun and excitement when their fantasy arouses.

The migrant workers normally finds themselves starved for sex, those migrant workers who migrate from rural villages to big urban town and city in search for work, or those who migrate to foreign countries in search for better job and business opportunities, these migrant workers are mostly youngsters in their mid-20s and 30s, they are mostly single unmarried or even if they are married they have to live their spouse at home as they can't afford to take them to the city or country they go for work. So, mostly these types of young migrant workers are deprived of sex and bodily pleasure.

The migrant workers mostly live in groups, if we talk about men migrant workers, they have to share small room or a two room apartment between 8 to

10 men, hence all these men who share same small cramped apartment very obviously they also have just one bathroom and toilet to share among themselves, also have to change clothes in front of each other as they have no privacy at all, hence these men becomes more and more frivolous, hence, when these men's libido is high, passion arouses, they feel desperate need for bodily pleasure someone to cling on too, that's when these men craving for pleasure can't control their emotions and starts naughty activity and passionately begins to indulge in bodily activity with someone from their group or to say roommate/roommates who are apparently men. No, I'll stop short of calling these male migrant workers who intimately indulges among themselves as Gay or Homosexual, it's just that circumstances compels them in such kind of activity, what some may say immoral bodily activities.

Like men like women, yes, even women and girls as well migrate to more prosperous cities and towns as well to foreign countries to seek better fortune to earn higher salaries, also there are young girls who as well travel away from their home and parents either for higher studies or degree course or for professional training purposes, so, these women and girls as well have to share small two or three room apartments with other fellow women and girls, or stay in women hostels, now these wannabe women and girls as well crave for sex and bodily pleasure, unable to find suitable man for full fledge romantic relation, these women as well have to share common washroom and have to change clothes etc in front of other women roommates, so, these women keep nothing personal or private, girls and women share everything from their emotions to their sexy undergarments with their fellow women roommates, and also when their libido is high these young women and girls become desperate for sex and intimate pleasure, they start with giggling and tickling each other, woman cracks funny sleazy jokes and tries to tickle fantasy of other women, passionate snuggle and hard pinches, tickle on vagina, spanks (Buttock slapping), when their passion is sufficiently arouse, these women as well frivolously indulges in intimate bodily activity. It is just that their desperation compels them to have same gender sex practice, here again we have to be more considerate and not term these types of activity of migrant women, and not call them lesbians.

To understand things in better perspective, with regards to men gender are more circumspect and stealth when it comes to their sexual orientation, men tends to prefer to keep things under wrap about his sexual antics, about his indulgence with same sex gender (man), as he worries it will be socially unacceptable, because most religious communities and in constitutions of several countries, disallows the practice of homosexuality, hence men prefer to keep his desire of liking to enjoy sex and to have bodily pleasure with another man or transgender a top secret.

But in contrast, the women gender's only thing that haunts women is the thought of getting unwanted pregnancy, beside this one thought of becoming an unmarried pregnant woman, otherwise women it seems are less worried about the society and the social consequences as far as her sexual orientation is concern, woman less concern and unperturbed frivolously indulges with other girls and women, in fact most girls right from the time they reach puberty, the girls starts to enjoy there vices with passion and persistence more vigorously than boys and men do.

People in relationships often don't ask each other to do certain things simply because they are too shy to bring it up. This goes for both Men and Women, we fear that our partner might think you are a bit too weird. Before you try out your "new thing," break the spell of routine outside of your sex life by doing something non-routine together.

Most of you should know that women have some pretty crazy **Sexual Fantasies** and you should also know that they are far more adventurous than men will EVER be. But what you might not know is that women REALLY WANT men to do some rather naughty things in the bedroom -- but they are just too damn shy to ask or admit it. Women seem so cute and delicate on the outside -- yet they are just raging sexual beasts on the inside.

When passion is immense nothing else matters; Most women likes too and prefers to have best of both world, they like to intimately indulge with man as well as woman.

Like hunger for food, starving for sex could be equally devastatingly frustrating; Desire discrepancy is one of the most common occurrences that lead couples to seek professional help. Sex counsellors and therapists as well as marriage counsellors frequently encounter couples with one partner less interested in sex than the other.

Imaging smelling good food you know that you cannot eat. This is probably a pleasant experience, if you've had enough other good food to eat lately. But it might be a painful experience if you were starving, or had long been living on a bland diet of rice and beans.

Similarly, being around attractive sexy people is often a pleasant experience, but probably feels quite different when it is clear to all that you have zero chance of attracting them, and if you feel severely deprived of satisfying sex. And while our society is rich enough that few starve for food anymore, wealth is much less able to prevent sexual starvation.

So our society has far more sex-starved than food-starved folks. Yet it is far more acceptable to publicly lament the plight of the food starved than the sex starved. Signalling compassion is not about helping the needy.

It is a fact that many modern couples see their sex life crowded out by the relentless demands of children, work pressures, not enough time alone -- and simply not enough time. Allowing your physical relationship to fall to the bottom of a frantic "to-do list," experts say, can lead to dissatisfaction, loneliness, separation, and even divorce.

Something very important to understand; This lack of sex is more than just a lack of physical attention... It goes deep into a woman's heart. I think in a normal marriage, a couple can fight about anything, but then they can make love and soothe the bad feelings... sort of like a rebirth -- a forgiving ritual. But when you are deprived of even that, bitterness and resentment and desperation accumulate. I have a husband who is a good guy, great father, good provider, but I have no lover. I'm angry about the wasted years, the years I could have been loving, but spent agonizing about why I was being deprived. It's so much more than sex. It's feeling wanted, and sexy and desired by the man that you are committed to for life.

As you can see, women have no corner on the low libido market. Maybe you're asking yourself, "If low sexual desire in men is commonplace, why are they so closed-mouthed about it?" That's a good question. When a woman lacks sexual desire, although it may be troubling to her, she's not likely to start questioning the core of her femininity. After all, she's almost supposed to have "headaches". Men, on the other hand, are thought to have only three things on their minds-sex, sex and more sex. To be disinterested in sex is to feel less than a man. Just thinking about low libido- let alone talking about it- strikes terror in men because it threatens the very foundation upon which their feelings of self-worth are based. No wonder they're tight-lipped. But make no mistake about it. There are millions of people- both women and men -who just don't feel turned on.

Now, it would one thing if these lust less men and women were married to each other; they could agree to go off into the sunset, basking in platonic bliss. But, as fate would have it, it rarely works that way. People with low sexual desire are generally married to partners who desperately yearn for more sexuality, intimacy, physical closeness, and connection. And this chasm between them- a desire discrepancy- spells trouble. How do I know?

Still, the partner who consistently refuses sex needs to examine his or her attitudes, according to several marriage and family therapist. If one member of a couple is avoiding sex because of simmering tension or unresolved differences, that person needs to communicate or risk undermining the relationship. In his book Passionate Marriage sex therapist David Schnarch argues that both partners in a relationship need to stand up for themselves and learn to ask for what they want -- in the bedroom and outside it. Interestingly, separate equals exciting.

Part of the problem may come down to a myth about sex itself. "Many people believe that they have to be overcome with desire before they have sex. I think in a long-term relationship, you just have to have a willingness to be sexual. You just need to respond to your partner's overtures. And the more frequently you have sex and it is satisfying, the more that reinforces your willingness to do it again." In other words, simply having sex can fuel desire and turn up the heat.

In addition, "sex is remarkably sensitive to what's happening in all areas of individual and family life," says therapist and relationships expert Judith Wallerstein. "Illness, especially surgery, as well as depression, worry, fatigue, and stress can affect a man and woman's intimate life." In fact, sex therapists agree that if physical or emotional issues of any type are taking a toll on your intimate life, you need to seek help. Among other things, doctors or therapists can effectively treat changes triggered by menopause and problems like impotence and premature ejaculation.

Chapter 3

Different people have different perception and conviction, these are defining moments, very evolving situation.

Man and woman to develop romantic and platonic relationship, normally play mind game, both subtly keeps each other guessing about other's motive, as both are suspicious about other's honesty.

Girls normally list out their priority about what type of man they want in their life, most girls and women want their boyfriend and husband to be handsome, highly educated, smart, affluent and rich with owning his own house and cars, whom these girls also describe as theirs "MR Right." well nothing wrong with whoever crave for the best deal, we all after all want best of everything in our life. These girls want all the good qualities in what they perceive as there "Mr Right" (prospective life partner --- husband), but little do such females cares about is whether they themselves have all the right attributes to become someone else's "Miss Right" (prospective - wife). Most people have this habit of hoping lot of goodies from others without realizing or bothering if they have anything better to offer others or have nothing much of their own to offer others in return.

Each one of us humans, our Life is always pregnant with many possibilities, which possibilities will play out when, that only time alone will prove.

As it is, that, Good Times potentially may not last forever, similar notion, Bad Times will never remain Bad forever.

Time is of essence, Time is precious and mightier, Time at times makes dramatic changes, which deeply and comprehensively alters the future of not just you but of coming generations, as well.

Fortunes are made and broken at will, many individuals rise from Rags to Riches, in matter of moments (Quickly), while on the other side, misfortune strikes without any apparent warning, people fall from grace to disgrace and from riches to rags. So, almost every citizen in the world is equally vulnerable.

Most people have for long been living with this myth and illusion, that person/persons of particular "Race, Region or Religion" are better Sex performer than many others. This is a myth and illusion of people who are naïve, it is and unfounded truth, Sex drive of man/woman (power to perform sex) has got nothing to do with what race, region or religious community he/she belongs to.

Don't simply go by the structure of a person's body, the body structure of a man may be strong hard muscular, girl's body as well if it looks smooth with dimple in her cheeks and over all beautiful and irresistible body, these sexy and muscular body structure is an external matter, Sex drive or strength to perform sex is something that's internal matter, so, sex drive depends fully on internal aspect and strength of a person. A strong and healthy men or soft and smooth skin ravishing women doesn't necessary mean he/she will be excellent on Bed,

It is always better to understand the psychology of humans from many different aspect and angle.

How most girls play mind game with guys; You all must have heard them, don't approach him first, don't flirt, don't look friendly, don't pick up the phone when he calls, wait at least four days before you call him back, never ever accept spontaneous invitation, act like you are not interested, don't show him if you like him, don't allow him to hold your hand until on the third date, don't introduce him to your friends until he introduces you to his, if he is not ready to commit when you are ready "Dump Him," never be friend with "ex" etc.

Who follows these types of rules? What kind of man a woman who follows these types of rules attract? It is possible to sustain a loving relationship based on a persona faking a busy life? What wrong with being an open, honest, vulnerable, proactive real woman with her own mind, a body and soul?

Every time we set up unrealistic, counter-productive and sometimes even ridiculous rules that assumes that all men and women reacts the same way to the same situation rather than that relationship is an interplay between two unique individuals, we set ourselves up for frustration, hurt and disillusion.

If all you attract is frustration, disappointment and hurt, change the way you approach dating and the way you relate to the opposite sex. Stop treat dating like a game or a necessary evil that you have to endure and instead see it a journey to discovery.

This is bit of humorous at Buzz-feed, but I know that many guys would call it 100% accurate. We call them jerks and douchebags, but we go for them anyway, don't we? If we didn't they'd be forced to stop acting so nasty to get laid. Do we force nice guys into last place?

I hear from a fair number of young men who are just as frustrated as many of you are in the search to find meaningful relationships.

The British have a saying: "Be mean, keep 'em keen." Why are we shooting ourselves in the foot time and again?

Why woman falls for guy who have poor attributes and quality; **Jerks have many qualities that are attractive to women.**

- There's the mystery surrounding a troubled soul or an enigmatic rebel.
- They exude confidence, though upon closer inspection it is really arrogance.
- They are extraverts.
- They have a lot of charm, i.e. player skills.
- They appear passionate. Usually, they are most passionate about fulfilling their own needs.
- Their intense pursuit is flattering and makes women feel special and desirable.

It's a challenge.

- Women feel that any love worth having should be earned first.
- They enjoy outplaying a guy (or trying to) at his own game.
- Jerks keep us guessing; we can't decipher them.
- On the flip side, nice guys are boring and predictable.

Women have a "fixer-upper" complex.

- They look into a guy's soul and see more than he is showing of himself, and they become hooked on the idea of getting him to open up.
- A flawed man gives this type of woman someone to work on and mould. They wind up viewing the jerk as someone who is misunderstood and unloved, a lurking lonely soul.

It's emotional.

- Women feel excited, disappointed, and confused. The rush of emotions is exciting and addictive.
- The process inevitably follows this pattern:

1. Jerk shows interest.

2. When woman returns interest, jerk draws back and appears nonchalant.
3. Jerk waits until woman is confused, then provides attention.
4. Repeat.

Weak women attract jerks.

- A jerk will not waste his time on a woman he knows respects herself. He preys on the vulnerable.
- It requires two parties with low self-esteem. The jerk uses a bad boy demeanour as his cover. His snide remarks and sarcasm are defence mechanisms.

<u>**Dating a jerk is the best way to avoid getting into a long-term relationship.**</u>

- Until you are ready to settle down with a sweet guy to have babies with, why not have fun with a jerk? Maybe even be a jerk?

<u>**It's a vicious cycle.**</u>

- Women are attracted to jerks, form relationships with them, and then try to justify their choice by seeing things in them that no one else can.

"They can be unpredictable, dishonest, or downright mean, but scoundrels have always had an undeniable appeal to us–an erotic edge of danger that's hard to resist."

As long as women choose jerks, there will be nice guys converting to jerkdom, especially if they've been dumped for a jerk. Nice guys who admit to employing this strategy don't like it much; they say it's exhausting to act like a jerk all the time. Let's give the nice guys a break. Look deeper. Don't settle. Respect yourself. All of womankind will thank you for it.

Do you resent women? Most men would respond of course not. They say no but chances are good that on some level they do resent women but just aren't aware of it.

Quite often bitterness for women goes on unconsciously, just below the surface. This is common even with men who are trying to get good with women. There are several reasons why this resentment exists:

1. Women can easily get sex

To some men sex is the end all be all of life. If they can't sleep with women they feel inadequate in many ways.

They feel extremely frustrated with life and with themselves from their lack of sex.

Unfortunately this frustration is often taken out on women. Their contempt for women stems from their anger at how easily women can get sex. It's a basic jealousy issue.

They will call women sluts or whores but the truth is they wish that *they could get laid as easily as women do.*

Their frustration is similar to how many poor people react to someone with money. They assume that the person is greedy or evil but really they are just frustrated by their own lack of success.

2. Women are able to get men to do whatever they want

When you feel completely powerless over your life the human thing to do is try to control others. When you can control and hold power over someone else you get a false sense of control over your own life.

Most beautiful women can control men with ease. They use their magical powers to get men to do whatever they want them to.

They will see women getting men to bend over backwards for them and they crave that. They thirst for the power women posses in order to feel powerful themselves.

Deeper than this is a desire to be loved. Controlling and powerless people have the crazy idea that *the more a person does for them the more a person loves them.*

Since most men are unsuccessful in attracting women, let alone getting them to do what they want, resentment builds. They despise these women but in reality they wish they could be in the same position as them.

Women complain that men do not contact them after the date because they're playing hard to get. But when they find a guy who shows them his true feelings and does not play hard to get they complain that he is too nice because he does not play hard to get. But when women start playing hard to get its frustrating to guys who are not interested in childish never ending games.

What we don't understand is, what is wrong in showing someone you love them? If man love a woman why can't he tell her how much he loves her and show her his feelings. Why say you need a man who can show his true feelings and at a same time want someone who plays hard to get? It sends lot of mixed signals.

Most people (men and women) interpret this as you are giving too much because you need too much. Most are turned off by the pressure to give back as much as they are getting. You do not need to verbalize that you want him/her to give you anything back in return, it just a given of life that when we get something we want to give something back to show our appreciation (for most "normal" people anyways). But when we get so much then we give back, as we feel the pressure.

If that man is lucky woman will tell him you are trying hard and need to step back a little.

Most psychological research concludes that person 'A' usually likes person B about as much as they think person B likes them. "If we want to know how much Debbie likes Steve, a good predictor is how much she thinks Steve likes her," write the authors of the paper, Erin R. Whitchurch and Timothy D. Wilson of the University of Virginia and Daniel T. Gilbert of Harvard University. "But what if Debbie is not sure how much Steve likes her?" This might lead Debbie to spend a lot of time thinking about Steve, wondering how he feels, and she may find him more attractive the more she dwells on those thoughts.

"Numerous popular books advise people not to display their affections too openly to a potential romantic partner and to instead appear choosy and selective," the authors write. Women in this study made their decisions based on very little information on the men — but in a situation not unlike meeting someone on an internet dating site, which is common these days.

"When people first meet, it may be that popular dating advice is correct: Keeping people in the dark about how much we like them will increase how much they think about us and will pique their interest."

Distinguishing yourself. That's the whole point of playing hard to get. Instead of being like the other needy girls, you act super cool and uninterested to stand out. You know what else would distinguish you? Giving better head than everyone else.

It makes sense to want to stand out from the crowd -- to do something to distinguish yourself. But why not *actually do something?* Be funnier, smarter, kinder, or, yes (even though it was a joke), better in bed. At least those are skills. Something tangible.

Article title "**Men are From Mars, Women are from Venus**" write: "Men love to have their abilities recognised and appreciated, and hate to have them scorned or ignored; women love to have their feelings recognised and appreciated, and hate to have them scorned or ignored. Men don't rate feelings highly as in their view they can result in hotly impassioned, wildly unstable behaviour; women don't rate abilities highly as in their view they can result in coldly dispassionate, aggressively competitive behaviour.

Men like to work on their own, and exercise their abilities by solving problems quickly and singlehandedly; women like to co-operate, and exercise their feelings through interactive communication with one another. Men value solutions, and view unsolicited assistance as undermining their effort to solve problems alone; women value assistance, and view unsolicited solutions as undermining their effort to proceed interactively. Men desire that their solutions will be appreciated; women desire that their assistance will be appreciated.

When faced with tough problems, men become non-communicative so they can work out how best to help themselves, while women become communicative so that others can work out how best to help them. Men like to demonstrate their abilities by being allowed to solve problems without interference; women like to demonstrate their feelings by being allowed to relate problems without interference.

When men do communicate, they like to get to the point, and generally only want to listen if they feel the conversation has a point; women enjoy talking for its own sake, and are happy to listen unconditionally.

How to Motivate the Opposite Sex;

A man's instinct is to look after himself, even if it means sacrificing others; a woman's instinct is to look after others, even if it means sacrificing herself. In a relationship, a man has to learn how to care for his partner rather than sacrificing her needs in favour of his own, and a woman has to learn how to be cared for by her partner rather than sacrificing her own needs in favour of his, so that the needs of both are met. If they do this successfully, both win, unlike their instinctive behaviours where one person gains from another's loss. This has to be worked at, because if either partner feels their efforts towards the relationship are not being successful in pleasing their partner, they may feel hurt and decide to revert to their instinctive behaviour. Unfortunately this then causes the other partner to do the same, and the relationship unravels inexorably.

In a relationship, a man needs to feel that his attentions are needed, and a woman needs to feel that her needs are attended. To achieve this, a man has to express his desire to fulfil her needs and her worthiness to receive his care, and a woman has to express her desire for his care and his worthiness to fulfil her needs. Both must remember to appreciate, accept, and forgive the other, and avoid blaming them when they fail.".........

Chapter 4

"One party can selfishly enjoy all the benefits of a relationship, the warmth and relief from loneliness, the satisfaction of the attention that feeds the ego — all without the accompanying commitment. One party luxuriates, while the other party feels cheated and is left with deep unsatisfied longings."

I've recently observed several non-dating relationships that seem to fall into the "intimate friends" category. In every case, it is the woman who is paying the price emotionally. Why? When a guy starts investing his heart, he can do something about it by making a move. And if the girl rejects him, the friendship ends or changes significantly. A woman, however, can hang on in this kind of relationship indefinitely, hoping the guy will eventually share her feelings. She makes herself available to him as a "friend," all the while hoping the friendship will blossom into something more.

Unfortunately, even if the guy senses the woman's interest, Maybe, we could chalk that up to communication differences between men and women: A man may be oblivious to unspoken signs that he has been placed in the "future husband" category. What he may be viewing as an innocent dinner, she sees as an indication that the friendship is developing into more. But men should assume that if a woman is spending a lot of time with him, she *is* interested and she *is* investing her emotions. (I suspect men realize this more often than they'll admit, but hold onto these ego-boosting relationships anyway.)

Women, on the other hand, need to assume less. A woman should not assume that a guy friend she's spending time with is: a) just too shy to make a move; b) thinking she's the woman of his dreams but the timing isn't right; c) in denial of God's will that they be together.

Song of Songs puts it this way, "Do not awaken love before it so desires." As a generation of women drunk on chick flicks, we want romance to happen so badly we allow ourselves to fantasize about relationships that have no founding.

Ecclesiastes croons, "There is a time for love." If, as a woman, you are indulging in an intimate friendship with a man who is not pursuing you, you are accepting a cheap imitation of love. And by spending all your time with a guy who will never put a ring on your finger, you may miss a potential suitor.

If, as a man, you are spending large quantities of time with a woman, you may want to consider if perhaps the relationship is deserving of an upgrade to an intentional relationship that explores the possibility of matrimony. If not, do your sister the courtesy of making your stance clear, freeing her to be pursued by another man.

"Involvement with people is always a very delicate thing.... It requires real maturity to get involved and not get all messed up."

--MANUAL OF ETIQUETTE—articulates: "Men often speak of good manners as *an accomplishment*. I speak of them as *a duty*. What, then, are good manners? Such manners as the usages of society have recognized as being agreeable to men. Such manners as take away rudeness, and remit to the brute creation all coarseness. There are a great many who feel that good manners are effeminate. They have a feeling that rude bluntness is a great deal more manly than good manners. It is a great deal more beastly. But when men are crowded in communities, the art of living together is no small art. How to diminish friction; how to promote ease of intercourse; how to make every part of a man's life contribute to the welfare and satisfaction of those around him; how to keep down offensive pride; how to banish the rasping of selfishness from the intercourse of men; how to move among men inspired by various and conflictive motives, and yet not have collisions -- this is the function of good manners.

Not only is the violation of good manners inexcusable on ordinary grounds, but it is sinful. When, therefore, parents and guardians and teachers would inspire the young with a desire for the manners of good society, it is not to be thought that they are accomplishments which may be accepted or rejected. Every man is bound to observe the laws of politeness. It is the expression of good-will and kindness. It promotes both beauty in the man who possesses it, and happiness in those who are about him. It is a religious duty, and should be a part of religious training.

There is a great deal of contempt expressed for what is called etiquette in society. Now and then there are elements of etiquette which perhaps might well be ridiculed; but in the main there is a just reason for all those customs which come under the head of etiquette. There is a reason which as regard to facility of intercourse. There is a reason in the avoidance of offense. There is a reason in comfort and happiness. And no man can afford to violate these unwritten customs of etiquette who wishes to act as a Christian gentleman."………

Some women are hesitant as well as feels insecure before sexual encounter, what advises to overcome anxiousness and follow bedroom etiquettes do experts have for those females to experience pleasure inside bedroom? What's your first instinct before you have sex? If it's to turn the lights off, you're not alone, says Debby Herbenick, PhD, author of *Because It Feels Good: A*

Woman's Guide to Sexual Pleasure and Satisfaction. "Many women are afraid of letting their partner see them naked with the lights on," she says. But here's the irony: "Most men love the way their partner looks—and they desperately want to see her naked, stretch marks and all!" Men are visual, she adds, and so keeping the lights off may take away a level of excitement for him.

Try a little candlelight or install a dimmer switch in your bedroom, suggests Dr. Herbenick. "Lights with a dimmer switch could be a great do-it-yourself project to suggest to one's husband, too. If he knows what the dimmer switch is for, he may jump on that project right away!"

Any woman who's heard a joke about female genitals "smelling like fish" may have thought to herself: "Yikes, do I really smell like that?" "Women get uptight about this," says Tina Tessina, PhD, a psychotherapist and author of *The Unofficial Guide to Dating Again.* "In addition, if your early background includes information that your sexual parts are 'dirty,' it can lead to fears about odour."

"The truth is, even healthy bodies have a scent," says Dr. Tessina. "This is actually a good thing, because your scent is your pheromones—those hormones that attract men. Yes, vaginal odour can get stronger in the presence of a yeast infection, but if you are healthy and clean, there's no need to worry. Any man who has had sex before is accustomed to the natural scent of sex, and it will even turn him on."

While you can take precautions like forgoing gassy foods before sex or taking anti-gas medication, Dr. Tessina suggests another route: "Develop a sense of humour about sex and about your body," she says. "Sharing a laugh during sex because someone had an 'eruption' can bring the two of you closer."

"Women, like men, often get hung up on performance anxiety," says Dr. Herbenick. *Does this feel good to him? Is he having a good time? Is he getting tired of this same old thing I always do?*

"If a woman is worried that she is bad at something about sex, she might let her partner know about her anxieties by saying something like 'I want to please you so much and I worry that I'm bad at oral sex' or 'I worry that I'm not very adventurous,'" she suggests. "This gives her partner the opportunity to reassure her of the ways that she does please him. Asking explicitly about what's working can help women to feel more reassured and confident about sex." Luke Vorstermans, a married man in Nova Scotia, Canada, says take heart. "Men are not nearly as complicated as women make them out to be," he says. "Since we're primarily visual and physical in our sexual expression, we're fairly easy to satisfy. And what really turns us on is when you get turned on. So instead of worrying about what turns us on, get turned on yourself."

The theory among sexual health experts: Women worry too much about whether they'll orgasm or not. "Although it's understandable that many women want to have an orgasm, the irony is that worrying too much about orgasm—and focusing very hard on it—can actually make it more difficult to orgasm," says Dr. Herbenick.

Now, in our world there are hundreds of millions of people for whom it doesn't matter if God exist or not, as they don't believe or care much in the concept of Religion, they are call atheist or agnostic, but, there are billions of people who resolutely believes in God and in the concept of Religion, and they profoundly with dedications practice their religious belief, whether Sex or professional business or family matters these religious people follow accordingly all the religious ritual. As we talk of and debate Sexual and Relationship matters it is not just human psychology that we need to discuss and understand but we also have to discuss sex and relationships matters from Religious, Physiological, Sociological perspective as well, Sex and relationship has also got lot to do with Science as well, so we need to understand sex from scientific angle as well.

To put things in perspective from Religion point of view, Article is "**sex Before Marriage**" writes; "**What does the Bible say about sex, unfaithfulness and casual sex?**

As we have seen, the Bible finds no problem with zestful sexual activity when the context is marriage. Take Genesis 2:24-25, for example. When a man leaves his father and mother and commits himself to his wife, the assumption is that they will become one flesh.

Or take Proverbs 5:18-19: "So be happy with ... the girl you married ... Let her charms keep you happy; let her surround you with her love" (GNB). Satisfying sex and marriage are happy bedfellows. Paul underlines this biblical principle. When he addresses the promiscuous Corinthians, he does not disallow sexual pleasure but he does place it in context: "Let each man have his own wife and each woman her own husband" (1 Cor. 7:2 JB). The implication is that within the bond of marriage sex is permitted, indeed expected and encouraged.

Why this emphasis on marriage? Paul gives the answer to that question in Ephesians 5:32, where he suggests that this mysterious fusion of two persons is intended to reflect the permanence of the union which exists between Christ and His bride, the church. Contemporary observations about the sex act seem to be saying something similar. It is now widely acknowledged that sexual intercourse between married partners transforms the individuality of the man and the woman. It welds the "I" and the "thou" into a new entity, the "we", without cancelling out the "I" or the "thou."

This unitive act is a pale reflection of the oneness which has always existed between the three members of the Trinity and which exists between Christ and the church.

If this is true, if this merging of two bodies symbolizes such permanence and depth, what happens when people sleep around."......

In an Article in "**Women Were Considered Ritually Unclean**": "*Through much of its history, especially in the West, women were considered ritually unclean.*
According to **Jewish tradition,** a woman's monthly flow of blood put her regularly into a state of ritual defilement.

Similar taboos against menstruation existed in pagan **Greek and Roman circles**. Through their anti-sex mania, **the Fathers** of the Church aggravated the fears of women's ritual uncleanness.

Church leaders were anxious that such uncleanness might **defile the holiness** of the church building, the sanctuary and mainly the altar. In a climate that increasingly looked on all aspects of sex and procreation as tainted with sin, **theologians** considered that an 'unclean creature' like a woman could not be entrusted with the care of God's sacred realities.

Prohibitions based on the presumed 'ritual uncleanness' of women have remained in **official Church Law** for the last 700 years.

Knowing this background, we need not be surprised to find that the vast majority of Fathers, canon lawyers, theologians and Church leaders were of the opinion that such a 'ritually unclean' person could not be entrusted with the ministry of the Eucharist. It is clear that this social and cultural bias invalidated their judgment as to the suitability of women for ordination."......

A taboo against women during pregnancy and menstruation was common among many nations in early pre-Christian centuries. Not only were women considered to be "impure" during these periods, but in danger of communicating their impurity to others.

"Contact with the monthly flux of women turns new wine sour, makes crops wither, kills grafts, dries seeds in gardens, causes the fruit of trees to fall off, dims the bright surface of mirrors, dulls the edge of steel and the gleam of ivory, kills bees, rusts iron and bronze, and causes a horrible smell to fill the air. Dogs who taste the blood become mad, and their bite becomes poisonous as in rabies. The Dead Sea, thick with salt, cannot be drawn as under except by a thread soaked in the poisonous fluid of the menstruous blood. A thread from an infected dress is sufficient. Linen, touched by the woman while boiling and washing it in water, turns black. So magical is the power of women during their monthly periods that they say that hailstorms and whirlwinds are driven away if menstrual fluid is exposed to the flashes of lightning" from **Pliny the Elder,** *Natural History*, **book 28, ch. 23, 78-80; book 7, ch. 65.**............

"**Is anal and oral sex between a married couple a sin**? Articulates: "In describing the decay of the Gentile society, Paul pointed out that it began with a rejection of God and the replacement of God with man-made idols made in the likeness of physical creatures (Romans 1:18-23). Without listening to God's definition of right and wrong, substituting their own desires in its place, it is not surprising that one of the first moral restraints to go was the restriction of sex to only married couples. "*Therefore God also gave them up to uncleanness, in the lusts of their hearts, to dishonour their bodies among themselves, who exchanged the truth of God for the lie, and worshiped and served the creature rather than the Creator, who is blessed forever. Amen*" (Romans 1:24-25). The problem is that after time, this becomes common place. Man gravitates toward new excitements and new sins. "*For this reason God gave them up to vile passions. For even their* women exchanged the natural use for what is against nature. Likewise also the men, leaving the natural use of the woman, burned in their lust for one another, men with men committing what is shameful, and receiving in themselves the penalty of their error which was due. And even as they did not like to retain God in their knowledge, God gave them over to a debased mind, to do those things which are not fitting" (Romans 1:26-28). The logical result of rejecting God and a freedom to have sex as man sees fit is experimentation in perverted forms of sex, such as homosexuality. I don't use the word "perverted" lightly. Paul points out that sex between two women or two men is not natural. In other words, the human body was not designed for homosexual sex.

Our own society has followed the same path that lead to the decay of the Gentile society. The popular slogan in the 1950's among intellectuals was "God is dead." By the 1960's we find a strong push toward "free love." Laws forbidding living together without marriage were abandoned in the 1970's. Then in the late 1970's to the present day we saw a strong push for the acceptance of homosexuality. Those practicing homosexuality cannot engaging in standard sexual intercourse since that requires both a male and female partner. So other forms of sex are substituted, such as anal or oral sex. Because of the increasing acceptance of homosexuality in the society at large, sexual practices that would never have crossed the average person's mind are now presented as legitimate alternatives."........

Article in **"Regarding the Ritual Bath after Sexual Intercourse"** throws light on Islamic religious ritual as in why a wash (Bath) is necessary:

"Why is it necessary to take a bath after indulging in sexual intercourse?

- Is it necessary to take a shower if orgasm has been achieved but there has been no intercourse?

- After sexual intercourse if the affected parts are thoroughly washed then,

    1. Is there still a need for a bath?

    2. If a person wears clean clothes without taking a bath, do these clothes become *napaak* (unclean)? That is can these clothes be worn after a bath to say the prayers?

3. If the answer to (2) is in the affirmative, then is it correct to assume that anything a person touches before taking a bath also becomes unclean and has to be washed?

- If only a small part of one's clothes get dirty due to body secretions as a result of sexual activity (with and/or without orgasm being achieved), can only this portion be washed to make the clothes *paak* (clean)?

- Is it correct to assume that body secretions as a result of sexual activity require a person to take a bath, normal activities of defecation only require the concerned parts to be washed and secretions like sweat as a result of heat/exercise do not require any special cleaning? If so, why?

As far as above questions, i.e. "why is it necessary to take a bath", is concerned, I think that its answer is quite simple. God has directed us to visit a house of His worship, or to participate in the very act of His worship with a clean heart and body. God does not accept any worship, which is without these two essential requirements. A clean heart means that the intention of the person should be nothing else but to earn the goodwill of God; while a clean body means that the person, under normal conditions should have performed ablution and after indulging in sexual intercourse should have taken a bath. This is how God wants us to worship Him. This is how He wants us to visit a house of His worship. This, in essence, is the decorum that the Ruler of the worlds has prescribed for us for times when we want to make ourselves present in His Court.

- The *Shari`ah* has prescribed a bath whether a person reaches orgasm without sexual intercourse or has indulged in sexual intercourse without reaching orgasm."................

Societies based on private property and competition, in which monogamous families became practical units for work and socialization, found it especially useful to establish this special status of women, something akin to a house slave in the matter of intimacy and oppression, and yet requiring, because of that intimacy, and long-term connection with children, a special patronization, which on occasion, especially in the face of a show of strength, could slip over into treatment as an equal. An oppression so private would turn out hard to uproot.

Earlier societies-in America and elsewhere-in which property was held in common and families were extensive and complicated, with aunts and uncles and grandmothers and grandfathers all living together, seemed to treat women more as equals than did the white societies that later overran them, bringing "civilization" and private property.

In the Zuni tribes of the Southwest, for instance, extended families- large clans- were based on the woman, whose husband came to live with her family. It was assumed that women owned the houses, and the fields belonged to the clans, and the women had equal rights to what was produced. A woman was more secure, because she was with her own family, and she could divorce the man when she wanted to, keeping their property.

Women in the Plains Indian tribes of the Midwest did not have farming duties but had a very important place in the tribe as healers, herbalists, and sometimes holy people who gave advice. When bands lost their male leaders, women would become chieftains. Women learned to shoot small bows, and they carried knives, because among the Sioux a woman was supposed to be able to defend herself against attack.

The puberty ceremony of the Sioux was such as to give pride to a young Sioux maiden:

Walk the good road, my daughter, and the buffalo herds wide and dark as cloud shadows moving over the prairie will follow you. Be dutiful, respectful, gentle and modest, my daughter. And proud walking. If the pride and the virtue of the women are lost, the spring will come but the buffalo trails will turn to grass. Be strong, with the warm, strong heart of the earth. No people goes down until their women are weak and dishonoured.

To understand sexuality from scientific perspective; " According to an article in **"The Science of Sexual Arousal"**: "Men and women experience sexual arousal very differently, not only physiologically but psychologically, according to researchers who are studying arousal using an array of new and refined methods.

One active area of research concerns cognitive factors that influence sexual arousal. In the mid-1980s, Boston University psychologist David Barlow, PhD, and his colleagues conducted a series of studies to examine the relationship between anxiety and sexual arousal. They found that men with and without sexual problems reacted very differently to anxiety-inducing threats of mild electric shock.

Men who reported having no trouble getting and maintaining erections, says Barlow, "would believe that they were going to get shocked if they didn't get aroused, so they would focus on the erotic scene." The result was that the threat of shock actually increased sexual arousal. But men who had sexual problems responded to the threat of shock very differently, says Barlow. "Their attention would be so focused on the negative outcomes that they wouldn't be able to process the erotic cues," he explains.

Since those initial studies, Barlow and his collaborators have been trying to tease apart the factors that distinguish men with and without sexual problems. One of the key differences, he says, is that men with sexual arousal problems tend to be less aware of how aroused they are.
Another difference has to do with how men react to instances when they can't become aroused, says Barlow. "Males who are able to get aroused fairly easily seem unfazed by occasions where they can't get aroused," he notes. "They tend to attribute it to benign external events--it was something they ate, or they're not getting enough sleep--not as characteristics of themselves." In contrast, men with arousal problems tend to do just the opposite, thinking of every instance of difficulty as a sign of a long-term internal problem, either physiological or psychological, he says.".........

Sexual arousal (also **sexual excitement**) is the arousal of sexual desire, during or in anticipation of sexual activity. A number of physiological responses occur in the body and mind as preparation for sex and continue during it. Genital responses are not the only changes, but noticeable and necessary for consensual and comfortable intercourse. Male arousal will lead to an erection and in female arousal, the body's response is engorged sexual tissues such as nipples, vulva, clitoris, vaginal walls and vaginal lubrication. Mental stimuli and physical stimuli such as touch, and the internal fluctuation of hormones, can influence sexual arousal.

Sexual arousal has several stages and may not lead to any actual sexual activity, beyond a mental arousal and the physiological changes that accompany it. Given sufficient sexual stimulation, sexual arousal in humans reaches its climax during an orgasm. It may also be pursued for its own sake, even in the absence of an orgasm.

There are several informalities, terms and phrases to describe sexual arousal including *horny, turned on, randy, steamy,* and *lustful.* Things that precipitate human sexual arousal are called **erotic stimuli**, colloquially known as **turn-ons**.

Article in **"Human sexual response cycle"** writes: "The **human sexual response cycle** is a four-stage model of physiological responses to sexual stimulation. Which, in order of their occurrence, are the excitement phase, plateau phase, orgasmic phase, and resolution phase. The cycle was first proposed by **William H. Masters and Virginia E. Johnson** in their 1966 book *Human Sexual Response.* Since then, other human sexual response models have been formulated.

Among both sexes, the excitement phase results in an increase in heart rate, breathing rate, and a rise in blood pressure. A survey in 2006 has found that sexual arousal in about 82% of young females and 52% of young males arises or is enhanced by direct stimulation of nipples, with only 7–8% reporting that it decreased their arousal. Vasocongestion of the skin, commonly referred to as the sex flush, will occur in approximately 50-75% of females and 25% of males. The sex flush tends to occur more often under warmer conditions and may not appear at all under cooler temperatures.

During the female sex flush, pinkish spots develop under the breasts, then spreads to the breasts, torso, face, hands, soles of the feet, and possibly over the entire body Vasocongestion is also responsible for the darkening of the clitoris and the walls of the vagina during sexual arousal. During the male sex flush, the coloration of the skin develops less consistently than in the female, but typically starts with the epigastrium (upper abdomen), spreads across the chest, then continues to the neck, face, forehead, back, and sometimes, shoulders and forearms. The sex flush typically disappears soon after orgasm occurs, but this may take up to two hours or so and, sometimes, intense sweating will occur simultaneously. The flush usually diminishes in reverse of the order in which it appeared.

An increase in muscle tone (myotonia) of certain muscle groups, occurring voluntarily and involuntarily, begins during this phase among both sexes. Also, the external anal sphincter may contract randomly upon contact (or later during orgasm without contact).

In males, the beginning of the excitement phase is observed when the penis becomes partially erect, often after only a few seconds of erotic stimulation. The erection may be partially lost and regained repeatedly during an extended excitement phase. Both testicles become drawn upward toward the perineum, notably in circumcised males where less skin is available to accommodate the erection. Also, the scrotum can tense and thicken during the erection process.

In females, the excitement phase can last from several minutes to several hours. The onset of vasocongestion results in swelling of the woman's clitoris, labia minora and vagina. The muscle that surrounds the vaginal opening grows tighter and the uterus elevates and grows in size. The vaginal walls begin to produce a lubricating organic liquid. Meanwhile, the breasts increase slightly in size and nipples become hardened and erect."………

Sex for many people around the world maybe just a simple physical bodily activity, that's how some folks perceives it, but not many are aware there is a deep science as well involve in sexual bodily pleasure, with many inherent risk of contracting diseases.

Since the first cases of AIDS were diagnosed sometime in the 1980s, the depiction of women in the scientific and political discourse of HIV/AIDS has dramatically transformed. Virtually invisible in the earliest phases of the US epidemic, then treated as stigmatized vectors of the virus, women were expected to protect themselves by insisting on male condom use—despite feminist recognition of the reasons this expectation would fail. More recently and remarkably, the primary face of AIDS is a woman from the global south—a face deserving both sympathy and support, if not rescue. Meanwhile, men who have sex with women remain a forgotten group in the epidemic, almost entirely unaddressed in HIV prevention programs.

How, why, and for whom did women become the primary vulnerable victims of the HIV epidemic? More important, does this transformation serve the current needs of those at risk for HIV? Here we consider the etiology and evolution of what we have termed the vulnerability paradigm, a model that has been latent within the research literature and policy lexicon, but a ubiquitous model that we wish to name explicitly. According to this paradigm, women are susceptible to HIV because of biological differences in susceptibility, reduced sexual autonomy, and men's sexual power and privilege. Conversely, heterosexual men are active transmitters of HIV but not active agents of prevention. The paradigm assumes not only that women (but not men) want to prevent HIV but lack the power to do so, but also that men are more likely than women to bring HIV into the partnership. The model tends to ignore how heterosexual men contracted HIV themselves and how variability in biosocial and cultural contexts influences women's and men's probability of infection if exposed.

To be sure, both biological susceptibility and gendered power dynamics drastically disadvantage women worldwide. However, the vulnerability paradigm can also mask women's power and agency. Moreover, the model assumes that women want to protect themselves, but men do not. Similarly, men, but not women, are presumed to engage deliberately in risky practices. Finally, the paradigm applies gendered, structural understandings and interventions to women's behaviours but not to men's, especially heterosexual men's. Upwards of 70% of transmissions worldwide are now between a man and a woman, but programs and policies largely fail to include the prevention needs of men who have sex with women.

Although women's greater biological susceptibility is now well accepted, this was not assumed early in the epidemic, when the vagina, as opposed to the anus, was thought by scientists to be a rugged tissue that protected women from infection.

Sadly but true, a very disturbing fact, that overwhelming number of people, it will be safe to assume that all those folks who practice intimate bodily pleasure be "Gay or Straight" literate or illiterates do not follow adequate safety procedures, as they have scant knowledge and understanding of potential inherent risk involve in sexual activity, even the most intelligent and sensible person/persons goofs up big time in the bedroom before and after experiencing sexual activities, we all agree that sex is the most fascinating and entertaining physical bodily activity, sex gives us pleasure like nothing else could, but people fail to understand that sex is No child game, reckless and feckless indulgences in sexual activity whether with sex toys or masturbation, or full physical bodily activity between two opposite sex gender could potentially have dangerous consequences.

It is so important for women to throughout her life take outmost care of her most pivotal organ of her body "Vagina" as if those women who are not taking adequate precautions of keeping their vagina clean hygiene and healthy thereby those women are not only risking their own health but potentially transmit disease to her partner whom she may have sex with, particularly those couples who practice Oral Sex and Anal Sex. Most women are taught early on to cleanse daily with strong soap or use "feminine hygiene" sprays, but this can actually do more harm than good. Knowing the right way to stay clean, choosing foods that will boost your health, and even exercising your vagina are all ways you can keep your vagina in tip top shape.

It may seem counterintuitive, but washing your vagina with soap, whether its bar soap or liquid, isn't the best way to keep clean. The vagina actually stays quite clean on its own without the help of outside cleansers. Like other parts of the body, the vagina has a pH level that needs to be maintained within a certain range - 3.5 and 4.5, to be specific - in order to prevent the growth of unhealthy bacteria and facilitate the growth of good bacteria. Using harsh cleansers can upset the balance, leading to infection, irritation, and even bad smells.

As, it is important to have sex but it's also important to follow some sexual hygiene habits too. Poor hygiene can lead to infection which in turn can lead to serious diseases. So, get innovative and sassy under the sheets, but follow certain sexual hygiene habits to have lots of safe sex!

For good health and hygiene purpose it is important for women, it is essential to note the direction of washing your genitals. It is recommended to wash from your vagina to your anus to prevent the transfer of germs from the anus to the vagina and also avoid yeast infections.

Also, Both partners should wash their hands and nails before and after sex to prevent transfer of germs and bacteria to your genitals. Ensure, it is important to trim the hair in the private parts. During summer, heat and sweat can result in boils and skin problems.

Especially for women and girls, to avoid embarrassment or bad odour, women should avoid having sex in the first two days of their menstrual cycle. "Avoid oral sex if your partner has sores around the mouth or near the genitals, it can pass on to you."

Evaluating Sex and Relationship by analysing the "Scientific, psychology, physiology and sociology" angle, which proves that it is of paramount important that for healthy sex and happiness and unity of family relationship, good hygiene and healthcare is extreme necessary.

But, to manage and maintain extreme hygiene and healthcare, we also need appropriate civic infrastructure with all basic amnesties available to the masses all over the world, so, is the world fully equipped with basic civic amnesties, Is our social sector fully entrenched? The answer is a big "No," at least in 70% of the world countries civic infrastructure is in a disarray and in appalling condition. Which apparently has made life of humans in most civilian societies a nightmarish experience or to say it is structural discrimination against humans.

Who is responsible for such appalling civic infrastructure? To large extent the citizens themselves but the bigger and biggest reason for the plight of dismal public healthcare system and poor civic infrastructure is the flawed political system. It needs critical thinking with practical and pragmatic assessment of the ground reality of real world issues.

Since the 1980s most of the politicians who apparently also are responsible for running the country's government have adopted a rather bizarre and callous Capitalist style of economic and political system. Hence paying little or no attention towards social sector and public welfare, without elaborating much but in brief I would like to point out, that, increasingly almost all major and prominent countries politicians are fully focused on Capital Markets (stock market), lots of sops in terms of printing unprecedented amount of cash money to make credit easily available to the voracious bankers and stockbrokers with an objective of boosting stock-markets indices and stock-values for the benefits of select few rich and powerful people, with rising Stock indices and companies stock prices select few corrupt and perverts politicians and businessmen's are making oodles of money, millionaires have become billionaires.

The social sector welfare and improvement has been left behind, what the world's citizens needs is **Not** solid economic reforms but healthy and comprehensive social sector reforms, which will ultimately improve the living standards of common-man, Human minds has creativity. When citizens and bureaucrats get together then by discussions and by using their creativity most problems can be solved. All that is required is to create a human mechanism or apparatus which can liberate the potential creativity, but, the policy makers "the bureaucrats and politicians," from every country but particularly the developing and under-developed nations simply talks and brags only fools the people of their respective countries, too much talk but to little or no action, only corrupt practices.

The problem is that the infrastructure (water, electricity supply, roads, drainage, sewers, schools, hospitals etc.) has not improved or increased at the same rate as the increase in the population. Consequently, residents of cities are facing the regular nightmare for lack of water and electricity, bad roads etc.

According to one of the reports prepared by Unicef, nearly 40% of the world's population lacks access to proper toilets. According to some estimate 6 in 10 Africans remain without access to proper toilet, poor sanitation threatens public health.

Sanitation is not a dirty word, sanitation matters, "Sanitation is a cornerstone of public health and wellbeing," sanitation has seriously lagged behind time, the absence of sanitation has severely impacted the health and social development of most people around the world. Sanitation facility provides person/persons safety and dignity.

Millions of girl child around the world are withdrawn from schools and colleges once they reach puberty, particularly hard hit girls are from Indian sub-continent countries like India, Pakistan, Bangladesh and Afghanistan also girl child in countries of Africa are most impacted, because the schools and colleges in most of these countries are not equipped to provide clean water and soaps to young girls to wash themselves and to maintain high degree of hygiene.

One problem adds to another problem, each different problems have multiplier effects on civil society, it just keeps adding up, and so keeps increasing ordeal of most of the people and lives them to deal with excruciating challenges.

If Sanitation is big issue, than, healthcare and housing are even bigger problems that humans are dealing with almost all over the world.

Hundreds of millions of people are homeless and almost half the world's population are deprived off and can't afford good quality healthcare, as in most countries there is acute shortages of trained medical professionals as well as healthcare centres and hospitals. Basic lifesaving medicines so critical for the survival of us (humans), are, so much expensive that it has become beyond the reach of most of the people around the world, not just critical lifesaving medicines even the most basic medicines like cough syrup, eyes and nose drops are the medicine so pricey that many individuals can't afford to buy. These are matters of profound concern as so many people are losing their life for the want of basic medical healthcare.

Malnutrition is another big concern and so is obesity, nearly 1.2 Billion people around the world either are under-nourished or morbidly obese, such people can't enjoy their life as state of their health restrict them from many physical activities, neither can they do professional work nor can they enjoy extra curricula fun. According to some estimates there are hundreds of millions of people in our world who either gets very little food to eat everyday of their life or in extreme case suffers hunger, while starvation is a big problem, obesity stigmatized persons impacted by it, people who are obese suffers from some of the most brutal health problems.

Now, while on one hand there is a problem of starvation and undernourishment, than on the other hand it's the obesity that's rising at alarming rate around the world, but there is also altogether different type of health problem call **Anorexia**.

Anorexia is basically women related health problem, as almost all the victims of anorexia are women very few are men, the victim of anorexia are not economically weak or poor, but, most of the women and young girls suffering from anorexia are from well to do middle class or upper middle class families for whom money is not a problem, girls feels peers pressure, to maintain their looks and restrict weight gain so as to maintain their waistline, to remain slim and trim. Most girls who suffers from anorexia are from fashion and glamour industry, the girls (mainly, fashion models and movie actresses) feels that the slimmer is their body, the more the chance for them to securing modelling assignments, hence, immoderate food restriction, inappropriate eating habits or rituals, obsession with having a thin figure, and an irrational fear of weight gain.

Well, it simply doesn't makes any sense to remain physically fit you have to deliberately starve yourself, or resort to any kinds of doping habits like smoking cigarettes etc, adopting such manner and methods to control weight gain only leads to further health conundrum, it only increases the medical bills and healthcare cost. Not only does starvation results in physical complications, but mental complications as well.

With due respect from me to the medical professionals, the Doctors and whole Scientific community for doing the most appreciating job of helping humans in every aspect of life, by your dedicated and determined effort in research of medicine and tireless work, you all have helped us humans to survive in this world, there are significantly large percentage of doctors who are honest and fully committed and their integrity towards medical profession cannot be doubted. But, sadly with heavy heart I am compel to write, I would like to point out that overwhelming percentage of doctors and medical professionals across the demographics are not trustworthy, call them cheats, quacks or fakes, these doctors have scant or incomprehensible knowledge and understanding of medicine and health related issues, they are money minded, and also according to some media reports these so-called doctors or quacks are also serious sex offenders are accused of sexually exploiting their patients and worse still have been found to be involve in humans organs pilferage and smuggling.

Poverty is biggest crux of it all, all over the world approximate an estimate suggest that nearly 800 Million people are living under acute poverty and most among them are homeless. Hundreds of millions of people are compel to live in shanty localities in slums under most excruciating squalid living condition.

Housing is such a big problem, to enjoy life and to live a healthy sex life, one needs a clean environment, but most people are so hard pressed and poverty stricken that they can't find peaceful place to enjoy sexual activities. Whether we talk of developed or under developed countries or cities, particularly talking about the Asian communities which has an age old tradition of staying in joint family, in joint family culture where all members of the family stay under one roof, but, what binds such families, together? Culture, tradition and emotion have become less of an issue, it is more of an economical reason, as most of the Sons from the joint families does not or can't earn enough money to buy home for himself and stay separately on his own away from his parents and siblings, that is what becomes catalyst for the families to stay united as cost of living and survival becomes more manageable.

But the reality of joint families is a sordid tale, whether it is in Indian Sub-continent countries or even develop countries like England or U.S.A, most joint families have to share 2 or maybe in some case 3 room apartment or house among 10 to 14 family members, yes, most of the Asian communities or for that matter any other regions ethnic communities as well who believes in joint family culture, are normally large size, mostly they may number varying from anything between 8 to 25 members in a particular family, now what happens is that when such large families live united in 2 or 3 room house, the brothers and their respective wives have to make many adjustment and compromises of their personal interest as well as their dignity.

In joint families, the family members are mostly hard pressed for living space, hence the brothers and their wives have to share bedroom in turns, in some of the houses they have to work out some extraordinary methods, wherein brothers simultaneously have to share the same bedroom at night with just a fabric curtain partitioning the room. As desperate time calls for desperate measures, hence humans find some workable solution for any or most of their problems. One should not forget to laugh even in adversities as well in awful situations in which their life has thrown them into. **The power of thoughts after all, is what separates humans from wild life (animals).**

Here, I would like to comment, that all the problems and quandary of humans are self-made, no point whatsoever in blaming others for your plight, you are equally responsible for your ordeal, it's just that we've made it our habit to accuse others to hide our own mistakes, yes, it is an undeniable fact world over overwhelming majority of politicians and businessmen are corrupt but after all they as well are one among us they as well are humans, it is we the people after all who elect or select these politicians and business honchos to lead us.

Chapter 5

Love is one of the most profound emotions known to human beings. For some, romantic relationships are the most meaningful element in their lives, providing a source of fulfilment outside of ourselves. But the ability to have a healthy, loving relationship is not all innate. Failed relationships happen, and most of us have to work consciously to master the skills necessary to make them flourish.

For most people, **romantic relationships** can be the most important part of their lives. Romantic relationships are often thought of as friendships with the addition of passion, intimacy and commitment.

To love and to be loved just as you are; to form a partnership and build a lifetime together; to look at your partner and see the future, these are some of the most rewarding parts of life.

But what goes into these romantic relationships? Why do some romantic relationships fail while others thrive? What makes up a healthy relationship? Is what's healthy for you healthy for another? Let's explore romantic relationships a bit.

Here's the real truth about human relationships: **MOST OF US HAVE BEEN PROGRAMMED TO FAIL IN OUR RELATIONSHIPS**, no matter how much we want to succeed.

To make matters worse, much of what we've learned about relationships, from romance novels, TV, movies, or talking with friends--is just plain wrong!

The idea that two people meet, fall in love, and live happily ever after is one of the biggest myths ever perpetrated on Western civilization. The real truth is two people meet, fall in love, begin living together, and then do just about everything they can to diminish and destroy their love for each other.

Let's face it. You've got a better chance of surviving cancer today than you do of having a successful long-term relationship. This includes marriage, living with someone, business partnerships, and many other social unions.

Most people go through life without ever understanding the key elements that make their relationships succeed or fail. The purpose of writing this Book is to shed some light on this very important subject.

Sure, there are a few lucky souls who naturally succeed at interpersonal relationships. But that tiny group probably doesn't include you or me! If we're going to succeed in this challenging arena, we're going to have to do it the hard way. We're going to have to learn from our mistakes and find out what really works. Then we're going to have to stop doing the things that don't work and start doing more of the things that do.

Simply writing theories and through academic debates and discussion it is difficult to find solution to much deeper problems that is so gravely affecting peoples life the world over, to understand global level problems we have to view things from ground level perspective. The global population as per some estimate is well over 7 billion people, hence in different region and civilizations as well from different cultures and religions people have different perceptions and convictions. Hence we need to thoroughly scrutinise the ground reality, as, real life problems needs real time solutions.

Common sense is like a deodorant, those who needs most, they don't use it.

Who do you think really enjoys sexual life? Does the man who is rich and has lot of cash at his disposal, does he enjoys more sex, than to say a man who is poor and has no free cash money in his hands. Indeed, it is a known fact that rich men like the kings, prince, military dictators, rich businessmen are notoriously known to be womaniser, yes, the rich men with lots of cash can afford to have many luxuries for themselves, multiple wives, girlfriends and concubines etc, however true as it maybe, but not really, there are many rich folks as well who remain deprive of sex, and it is always not doom and gloom for those men who are financially weak (poor), their happens to be many men who otherwise are constraint of hard cash yet they get abundant sex in their life.

Most humans, men or women live their lives with multiple worries, especially with regards to their health and shape of their body's. most boys and men keeps worrying about their body, their height, muscles and weight, their Peni size particularly if they believe their Peni is too small, or about baldness when they lose their hair, about their height if they feel they are too short and their skin colour complexion when they feel their height is too short and skin colour is dark and they are not muscular enough to attract attention of girls, also their body weight gives them jitters. But, at least what I have observed myself is that significant number of males are not particularly worried or at least they don't show their concerns openly in their social circle and frivolously carry's on living their life.

Similarly like men, the female gender is not left far behind in their worries, girls and women are as well extremely concern about the size and shape of their body, but, the biggest concern that most young girls and women have is the size of their breasts/bosom, whether their breasts size is big or tiny – small, the shape and size of their breasts worries young women folks a lot, apart from breasts it's also the shape and size of their nose, their lips, how their expression looks when they smile, then, also about the waist line, hairline, neckline, shape and size of their butt (buttock), gosh this women gender have plenty of things to worry about, but above all, the concern for females is not only their own looks and style that they have to worry about, the women have inherited tendency of bothering about other girls and women as well, peers pressure - you see. Females are extremely focused towards their peers (other' women), they want to know and keeps track of, as in, what other females are up to, other females dress styles, hair styles, boyfriends and husbands, sex and relations, extramarital relation etc, etc, so female gender worry not just about themselves but spends considerable time and afford observing what's going on and what happening in other women's life as well, it just adds to their growing list of concerns.

Basically it has been observed that most women makes big blunder of trusting another woman. Because, in the opinion of many experts, "it is the woman who always misguides another woman."

As I reflected on how women talk about other women, I thought about what I've heard so many women say over the years. Most women will tell you that they have survived at least one mean girl in their past: a girl who dismissed, put down, or even socially tormented them. What does various research and experts, say? It probably goes without saying that the research is complex, particularly because it is challenging (or impossible?) to measure a critical, negative or hostile attitude given the self-serving bias that makes people want to see themselves as good and upstanding.

Research shows that women during the college years may have negative attitudes about particular types of other women. Few surveys have found that female college students were less likely to want to be friends with another female who was seen as sexually promiscuous, when compared to the rate for male college students who wanted to be friends with a promiscuous male peer. Various studies done have discovered "that the women clearly noticed the promiscuous woman and also had negative beliefs about her as a result."

In talking about the influence a mother has on her daughter, we also have to talk about **social learning theory**. Social learning theory reminds us that modelling has much to do with how children learn. The real but graphic truth is that there are many mothers out there in the world who aren't so sweet to their daughters, and readily say and do things that would make many of us cringe. It's critical to note that much of what is said and done by mothers that is ultimately hurtful was engaged under the veiled intention of having 'her best interests in mind.' I have found that women who are mean-spirited about other women were often raised by a mother who probably didn't like herself and didn't feel warmly toward women, in general, either.

As it is, the ground reality of life is a lot different and extremely complex.

Now, back to the same topic, as in, what young girls and women most worries about?

Young girls and women are outrageously worried about one thing and that is the size of their breasts or boobs or tits, call it by whatever word you think is suitable, whether the breasts size is big or small, girls fret a lot with regards to the size and shape of their breasts, particularly so are those girls who have very small tiny breasts, the girls and women whose breasts size is abnormally small it feels to them like a flat chested boy, yes, the girls who have small breasts seems to be lot insecure than as compare to girls who have large size breasts.

But, does the size of breasts really matters? It all depends, as, the women also construe their size of breasts from boys and men's point of view, what do young boys or even desperate old men like to see in the women?

Here I would like to add, I don't know, what other surveys or studies that have been conducted with regards to seeking opinions of boys and men as to what they prefer and like, do young boys and men likes girls with large breasts or small breast? See, I haven't really bothered to find out results of other surveys or studies, but, here is what I have discovered and what Male "friends and acquaintance" of mine have told me in private conversation, all through my life as many young boys and men that I've discussed with about what type and kind of girls and women they like seeing and would prefer most in their girlfriend or wife to have, the answer is 100% every boy and men have so far told me that they get most excited when they see a women who has large breasts, yes, my own personal research with regards to the size of women's breasts, every male folks have emphatically told me they love and like to see those girls the most who has/have large Breasts and Sexy Round Shape Butt and would also perhaps like their wife and or girlfriends if any as well to have a big breasts and sexy butt (buttock).

From what I understand is that most men overwhelmingly likes girls and women who have large breasts and fat buttock. From a men psyche and perspective, a women who has all filled up body that means big breasts and nice rounded shape fattish type of buttock (butt) looks in real sense femme fatale.

So, as we know, as it is common, that, most girls who have tiny small breasts either wears specially styled bra with lots of padding to give enhance look to her breasts, as well as, most women with small breasts also takes a more pragmatic step of going through surgery, cosmetic surgery to inflate their breast, well, whatsoever measures women tries and take to fake her breasts size, but she can't fool many people, most people are clever enough to understand what is real and what is artificial.

In some cases the breast of a women fully develops only once she gets pregnant, as it is breasts grow a lot (especially those milk glands) during pregnancy, so any woman who hasn't been pregnant doesn't YET have fully developed breasts. Breasts ONLY develops fully during a pregnancy, losing some fat and then the milk glands grow a lot during that time. Breasts may become larger during pregnancy, but, don't rejoice yet, there is a caveat, "Breasts generally revert to their approximately previous size after pregnancy, although they may so live increased sagging."

Again, my advice is that, those Women who have a large breasts you have good reasons to rejoice, because your large size breast will tempt more men to have look at you because you'll look sexy and seductive.

Women with small breasts, y'all should not unrelentingly worry about the size of your breasts, more so, instead should spend your quality time in enhancing professional skills and on improving your personality, because it is the skill and personality that will last forever and after all its the skills that you may have will make positive impact on your life.

Girls and women, who have large breasts, please don't temper with the parts of your body, this is how mother-nature has created you to be and to look like, as the nature has blessed you with naturally large breasts so live it the way it is, please don't try reducing it under some false and misleading advises, because, when you try to defy natures given gift to you, it more often than not proves fatalistic and can potentially harm your body and waste you hard earn money on medical bills.

For women with small breasts, respect what nature has given you, don't mess up your body simply to attract attention of few people and to look attractive in social circle, every kind and types of cosmetic surgery has its own side effects, you may potentially end up messing yours or your family's finances big time trying to artificially inflate your breasts or to that matter any other organs or parts of your body.

How can you love someone else if you do not love yourself first? Impossible, right? Exactly. Take note of your inner and outer beauty. If you do not like it, then you could change your hairstyle, hair colour, the way you dress, etc. Do not change your body parts because they look abnormal to you, or someone else's bigger than you. Everyone is different. Everyone is unique in their own way, and you are too! So keep your head up and think positive!

Alright, but, no stopping yet, a lot to discuss, not just girls and women fakes size of their breasts but most of these clever women in bedrooms also fakes orgasm.

Women fake orgasms? I hate to break it to you but yes, women do indeed fake orgasms, and have been doing so for quite some time now! But the more important question is: why do they fake orgasms? Before we get into the few potential reasons, why women fake orgasms? A look at the power of an **orgasm** might inform and influence some of us.

The orgasm is not only physically powerful for women, but also psychologically powerful for men, which is not surprising. Here is what we know about men when it comes to issues in the bedroom. A man will feel more like a man if he knows he can satisfy a woman's sexual needs. Of course, women know this, and realize the importance of boosting a man's confidence in the field of lovemaking. Orgasm equals sexual satisfaction equals an enhanced relationship. Hence, women often act out fake orgasms.

Women gets a little thrill from being able to control a guy's gradual climb to a climax. It is a feeling of power. The challenge comes in seeing how excited you can get your guy, and how long you can prolong his orgasm. The fact that a woman can get her guy off with a fake orgasm, whenever she feels like it, can be very satisfying.

Sad but true; sometimes women really are not in the mood and just want to get it over with. Again, so as not to bruise her man's ego, the woman will simply act out a fake orgasm in order to give her partner pleasure.

Although some people get aroused when there is some level of pain during **sex**, not all pain is good pain. If a woman is experiencing pain or discomfort during intercourse, it could be an indication that something is medically wrong. Nevertheless, she may simply fake it to bring things to an end more quickly rather than say something and spoil her mate's enthusiasm.

In some rare of the cases and instances, a woman faking orgasm can have profound psychological impact on her partner's (man's) mind, it could potentially make her partner impotent in extreme case scenario, hence husbands, boyfriends or paramours of woman ensure that your woman partner is seriously enjoying sex with you and not simply making artificial phoney gestures.

Now, about males insecurity, as it is, like women are gravely concern about the size of their breasts and nipples, the men gender profoundly worries about the size of his Peni, In fact, plenty of well-endowed men are ashamed of their penises, while lots of men with smaller penises strut their stuff with confidence, A man's level of anxiety about his penis size does not correlate to how his genitals actually measure up, that's what many studies have found.

It revealed that many well-endowed men worry about the size of their penis, while other less blessed blokes are confident in their assets. Men are far more concerned than women are by penis size.

Here again, the concerns of those men who are unduly worried with the size of their Peni, your reasons for concerns are unfounded, whether the size of your Peni is 4" inch or 6"inch long, it makes absolutely no difference on your power to have sexual pleasure, you will be able to entertain your partner (woman) as much with, whether you have 4" or 6"inch long size Peni.

Now, your external structure of the body no matter how so ever strong and solid it maybe, but, in case of both men and women it is the internal strength of your body which provides energy to you to perform sex.

Other thing that worries both men and women the most is, thought of impotency to every men and thought of infertility to women, just the thought of impotency and infertility makes men and women shiver and jittery.

If they are medically declared as impotent and infertile, it stigmatises both women and men, in society this is considered to be biggest taboo for the men to be impotent and women to be frigid and infertile and unfit for performing sex and unable to bear offspring.

Male impotence is also known as erectile dysfunction and is the lack of a person's physiological sexual ability. In this condition, a man suffers from the inability to develop or maintain an erection of the penis sufficient for satisfactory sexual performance.

Most men have scant knowledge of, what impotency is and what are the potential reasons/causes of impotency?

There are several reasons that can potentially make men impotent and women infertile, impotency is either a Temporary phenomenon as well as it could be Permanent, it all depends, as it majorly varies from person to person and radically differs on case by case basis, hence don't ever jump to conclusion ever so quickly, different person and individuals will have different results and outcome, depending upon each affected individuals "Medical history, age, physical health condition or Social and Domestic problems etc, etc," because it all depends, as in, what has caused impotency?

Most common reasons found to be cause for impotency in men are severe health problems like "Obesity, chronic severe headaches, diabetes, high blood pressure, fatal injuries caused by accident or could be psychological like depression due to job loss, debt repayments worries etc," such perilous matters and issues becomes major cause/reason for impotency in men, same with women as well, a women encumbered with stress and worries, or having health problems like diabetes, fatal injuries, cancer or any types of severe physical difficulty (handicap), than unhealthy eating habits, insalubrious diet etc can make a women infertile. Also the Aging factor plays in for both men and women, also I would like to point out other serious reason which is environmental reason, living in city and country where the pollution level is abnormally high and Air is dirty it could as well seriously affect its citizens Sex Life. (Note: Depending upon, Once an affected person's "Health problems or Personal problems gets resolve and sorted out," highly likely the affected person would potentially regain Back his/her Strength to perform normal sexual activity).

It is always nice to eat nutritional and healthy food, do regular exercises to remain physically fit, it will be immensely beneficial for both men and women. Even more important is and which will prove incredibly beneficial to every one of us, that is our own Positive approach towards our life, So, I strongly advice you folks, always, Never allow any kind of Negative thoughts and feelings if any you may have to override your normal Thought Process/your Mind, hence, Friends for you to live a happy life, "Be Positive, Think, Talk and Behave Positively" it will help you perform sex better, and will overall boost your confidence which help you live longer, healthy and wealthy.

But, remember, that, impotency and infertility is callous and such a type of menace that it does not distinguish between individuals and never discriminates between affluent class or underclass, race, region or religions, it spares no one, impotency and infertility could strike a man or woman at the time of its own choice, there is very little or nothing one can do about it to prevent it from happening.

Again to sort out impotency problems people try different methods, as medical science has made significant progress hence there are fertility treatments available for both men and women, but, again each medical treatments are extremely pricey and time consuming, also fertility treatments as well has potential risk of side-effects.

Talking about breasts and Peni sizes and impotency, now, what is most common sex practice? Vagina sex, oral sex or anal sex, it will be difficult for us to get correct figures or even estimates, as in, world over what kind of sex people indulges the most, however one thing is clear that most unmarried couple in heterosexual relationship, to avoid the woman from becoming pregnant mostly indulges intimately in anal and or oral sex as most preferred choice of physical sexual activity, that's because it helps the cause of woman especially if the woman is from socially conservative society wherein unmarried woman becoming pregnant is greatest stigma and taboo.

We can also assume that those homosexual couples or individuals by nature of the preference for their sex has no other better option but to satisfy their fantasies by indulging in oral or anal sex, even if they play with sex toys.

Otherwise in heterosexual couples, be it, the promiscuous men and women involve in illicit relationships or legally married men and women, circumstances compel most heterosexual couples as well for wide variety of reasons to avoid vagina sex and instead indulge in oral or anal sex.

"(Note: Men and Women (gay or straight) it is strongly advised to you all, that before indulging in "oral or anal" sex ensure both the partners are maintaining hygiene and have washed their body, more so, if either one of the partner or if both the partners are suffering from any kind of serious health problems like for example: have "Mouth ulcer, cancer, severe cold or cough or any kind of infection," in such cases and instances please avoid oral and anal sex altogether or even if you want to indulge consult experts take medical advice from your doctor, if adequate precaution and safety measures are not taken, both partners may potentially will be risking their health and could likely contract disease)."

So let us understand in detail as to what exactly oral and anal sex is. Oral sex is sexual activity between partners in which someone's genitals – penis, testicles, vulva (vagina, clitoris, labia) or anus -- are being stimulated by someone else's mouth, lips or tongue.

Names for some common oral sex activities are cunnilingus -- giving a person with a vulva/vagina oral sex, often colloquially called "eating out," or "going down on," -- fellatio -- giving a person with a penis oral sex, often colloquially called "giving head," or a "blowjob" – and analingus -- stimulating the anus of a person of any gender with the mouth, lips or tongue, often colloquially called "rimming."

Article title "**Anal Sex Play: How Safe Is Analingus (Oral Anal Sex)**? Has written "Many couples of various ages, religions and sexual orientations enjoy exploring their sexuality together. This may be particularly true for two people who have been together for a long time, are monogamous (and therefore fairly confident that they are not putting each other at risk for unknown infections by having sex with others), and feel comfortable with each other.

Comfort and trust are often critical factors since sexual exploration can pose potential emotional and physical risks as well as benefits.

Many Ways, To Explore Anal Sex Play
There are many ways to explore anal sex play. Some people use their fingers to touch the outside of the anal openings; others insert their fingers. Similarly, some people enjoy oral-anal contact (often called "rimming" or "analingus") either by licking the opening of the anus or inserting one's tongue.

Anal intercourse, which some people may more commonly think of "anal sex", typically refers to inserting a penis or sex toy into a partner's anus.
Like other sex acts, some (but not all) people enjoy anal sex play. It is important for couples to talk to each other about what feels good, comfortable and what you do want to do (or stop doing)."…………

Wow, Sex is such an amazingly beautiful thing that nature has thought us. But, I've overheard many people saying that, sex is cheap and vulgar. Well I have this to say to those people who hold such views about sex, Sex is not vulgar or cheap, it is the nefarious motives of those wicked individuals who discriminates sexual activities and practice it to exploit people, to say to least.

We see, listen and hear a lot about people faking their orgasm and their beauty apart from faking their emotions, so many fakes and cheats. How to find a true loving and honest persons? Always, very difficult, but certain precautions and awareness can save you from becoming victim of evil design of a narcissistic person/persons.

To make relationship a success and to enjoy the pleasure of sex, people should be willing to sacrifice their own interest, be more accommodative, be considerate, don't do trade off of favours, do not follow the **"give and take policy"** principles, meaning, you do favour for me and expect me to return back favour to you, you do bad to me and expect me to be equally bad to you, such give and take measures and methods leads to confrontations and only increases and widens differences, so avoid it "in any relationships" if you can.

There should always be two ways conversation, that means when man and woman are trying to workout loving relationship between them or matchmaking, always ensure that both man and woman are talking equally, more often, either of the two be it woman or man, do a lot of talking and gives little chance to other to talk, or one of the two deliberately keeps Quite and only let the other person do all the talking, one of the two seeks more information from other while giving little or no information about him/her.

Also we read and have been listening a lot about honour killings, normally it has been seen in 90% of the honour killing cases it is the women who becomes victim, and the main reason behind this brutal crime is that the daughter dares and defies her parents and chooses the life partner or spouse for her of her own choice, more often her chosen partner is from different religion or fraternity, that's what irks her parents and relatives hence they take extreme step of brutality and eliminate their daughter, that's how girls and women suffers.

Now, for generations, people are living with this myth and firm belief that the best recipe of successful marriage and relationship is to marry within our own ethnic group and same religious community or someone from our own fraternity, hence untiringly advocates the concept of marriage between man and woman from their own Race, Religion and Linguistic community. Such belief and perception are unfounded truth, if we do a thorough scrutiny and reality check it becomes evident and there's empirical evidence that throughout and across demographics most of the marriages that ended on bitter note, many incidents of turbulent marriages as well as nasty relationship break-ups and brutal end of marriages in bitter divorce, yes, overwhelming numbers of such instances have happen of relationship breaking and troublesome marriages despite the fact that both man and woman belonged to the same religious community, equal social strata and or from same fraternity.

So the success and failure or the durability of marriage and relationships have got nothing to do with whether or not you marry a person from within same Race, Religion or Linguistic community, whether they are socially conservative, devoutly practising religious persons, or have liberal social value of living life.

The success overwhelmingly depends on how honest and how much determine are both man and woman to make their marriage and relationship a great success story.

The purpose is to give a genuine solution to both men and women so as to make this bitterly divided and polarize world a better and safe place to live in and for the humanity to survive on this planet "Earth."

The fun is not in learning big things in life, but, the beauty is in understanding small things about life.

You won't become intelligent by thinking and trying to do big things in life, but, you will become more sensible and humble when you start caring about basic small things about life.

So, as we take our life more seriously, it comes to our understanding the significant of small things, small things makes big impact on us, hence from women perspective, whether they step out to find a job for themselves or they try to build up their professional career, even, whether in social circle or to find love or husband for themselves, what significantly matters the most is how well a women dresses herself.

As compare to men, women always needs to ensure that she is appropriately dressed for the occasion, because women's personality and acceptability in society depends on how well she dresses herself.

Vibrant colour and quality of fabric normally enhance women's look, women wearing provocative and skimpy clothes to look stunning per se doesn't augur to well, as wearing skimpy clothes she potentially risk her own safety and security. Women wearing shirt and trouser with boy-cut hairstyle will make her look like a man, woman always looks more gracious when she's dressed in traditional attire, every woman must ensure her clothes she's wearing makes her look feminine, women should look more and more womanish.

Another matter of critical importance is what type and kind of undergarment women wears, most women around the globe allegedly are less concern and cares little about the kind and types of undergarments (bra & Panty) they wear, they think their undergarments are fully covered and will not be seen by anyone, this is where most women makes big mistake, it is alleged that many women continue wearing same pair of undergarments (bra & Panty) for protracted period of time for 4 to 5 days without a wash at a stretch, such women inadvertently are not only negatively impacting their looks but also harming their health, because wearing undergarments without a wash for longer than normal period of time could potentially affect their health and make them sick.

Hence, it is of paramount important that women should always wear neat clean and good quality undergarments or to say lingerie regularly, not many are aware, but women's beauty and personality depends largely on how good a quality of undergarments she's wearing, wearing a quality undergarments (bra & Panty) will make that woman feel comfortable when she sees herself in mirror she will find herself looking sexy and seductive which makes her feel like a beauty queen, that feeling of a woman will change her mood positively and when her inner feelings will be full of satisfaction, it will reflect on her outer beauty, hence wearing a quality lingerie will make woman look attractive when she steps out of her house, that's why women appearing in public donning sexy good quality lingerie will have pleasant and appealing personality than compare to those women who trivialises the concept of donning good quality undergarments.

That's, why, it is always so important for people to understand small basic things in life, before we venture ourselves into adventures of life to play big risky games, we should first learn to get our basics right and rightly define our priorities.

What are those most critical aspects, that both men and women should look into, before they commit to each other, before they take the matter to next level and fall in love and become spouse and life partner?

From women's perspective, every women should ensure that the man who they want to fall in love with and intends to become his life partner, these are the few important things she should be careful of and needs to do. "The men/males always talks with high emotions and drama to impact the minds and hearts of women and girls, men are good at bragging and in boasting about their image, finances, etc, boys and men are clever, they know very well the art of bluffing their way in and out of relationship whether its romantic or intimate, men are good at bluffing their female partners, so, women needs to be smart, every woman before falling in love with a man, and making room for him in your heart and all the more important before you surrender your body to him, it will be in your interest to verify everything the man has told you and informed you about him, verify, what his religion is, truth about his finances about his family, don't make a mistake of allowing a man to play with your body unless you are satisfied about his motives, and you are convince about the man won't cheat you. This will save you and ensure you get a right choice and a genuine love and trusted life partner."

From men's perspective, men should also ensure he's not getting trapped and conned by a woman. "It will be in the interest of men to conserve their financial resources, men and boys should never over spend on dating with woman, men should restrain themselves from spending hard earn money on gifting expensive gifts to girlfriend or fiancée, as well on taking her out for lavish lunch and dinner or on picnics etc, boys and men should understand that most girls are sly, some of the women becomes friendly with men's simply to ensure that her man or boyfriend takes care of her personal private expenses gives her gifts and regularly takes her out for an outing, most women and girls are good at shedding crocodile tears, men's on their part should not succumb to such pressure tactics of women as more often than not women sheds crocodile tears to have her way."

I would like to reiterate myself, for all of us **"life is pregnant with many possibilities, which possibilities will play out when time alone will tell,"** women and men if y'all are seriously interested in having desirous love (romance) in your life and in romantic relationship, both, women and men needs to change their mind-set, needs to think more rationally, needs to become less finicky and less punctilious about your choice of "man or woman" and characteristics of the man/woman you want to have liaison with. As it is we are living in an uncertain times, your beauty will dissipate in matter of moments, wealth will evaporate without any warning, Master's degree and certificate becomes obsolete as there aren't many high paying corporate jobs available. So, tone down your rhetoric and bring down your high expectations and accepts relationship without much of a fuss, or you will be left alone in this world.

Invest your time and money in a person who has desire to do something, and not in a person who has passion to do something, here, we are discussing and debating about sex and relationship, so in same context of sex and relationship, look for a partner who has desire to be in romantic relationship or marry you, a person with desire will be more committed, accommodative and tolerant in relationship with you, in good times and bad times will remain with you, whereas a person he/she who has passion to be in relationship with you or intending to marry you, he/she will initially give big talks and commitments make tall promises, but, once his/hers passion will die down, he/she will snap ties with you and run away from relationship.

Certain precautions if both men and women (gay or straight) takes, that, will ultimately help both men and women folks find true love and ever lasting relationships.

Smart people learn from their own mistakes, but, smarter/smartest person/persons learns from others mistakes.

No matter how good an orator you are, how good is your communication skills and proficiency in language/languages you may have. But, what actually will save you from many troubles of life is a **Good Listening Skills**, yes, most people invites unnecessary troubles in their life as well as many family's gets disintegrate because of **Bad Listening Skills**. **Good Listening Skills** is a Master's Art, unfortunately most don't know the great significance of **Listening Skills.**

People around the world become victim of Propaganda, because they are **NOT** Intellectually Competent.

What people need to have the most? It is to have a quality **"Analytical Skills,"** to solve complex and uncomplicated problems.

It's Better to Walk alone, than with a crowd going in the Wrong Direction.

www.ingramcontent.com/pod-product-compliance
Lightning Source LLC
Chambersburg PA
CBHW071103290526
45795CB00004B/1641